Baccarat

JEAN-LOUIS CURTIS
ACADÉMIE FRANÇAISE

Baccarat

PICTURE RESEARCH AND
TECHNICAL CONTRIBUTIONS BY

VÉRONIQUE NANSENET

PHOTOGRAPHS BY
JACQUES BOULAY AND JEAN-MICHEL TARDY

HARRY N. ABRAMS, INC., PUBLISHERS, NEW YORK

"The Story of Baccarat" translated from the French
by Ruth Sharman

Library of Congress Cataloging-in-Publication Data

Curtis, Jean-Louis.
    [Baccarat. English]
    Baccarat / by Jean-Louis Curtis ; commentaries by Véronique
Nansenet ; photographs by Jacques Boulay and Jean-Michel Tardy.
        p.   cm.
    Translation of: Baccarat.
    ISBN 0–8109–3122–2
    1. Compagnie des cristalleries de Baccarat. 2. Crystal glass—
France—History—19th century. 3. Crystal glass—France—
History—20th century.   I. Title.
NK5205.C65C813   1992
748.294'3823—dc20   92–10479
                                                                      CIP

English translation of "The Story of Baccarat" copyright
© 1992 Thames and Hudson Ltd, London, and
Harry N. Abrams, Inc., New York
Copyright © 1991 Editions du Regard, Paris

Published in 1992 by Harry N. Abrams, Incorporated,
New York
A Times Mirror Company
Printed and bound in Spain

CONTENTS

Page 2. The River Meurthe, near the Baccarat crystalworks. In the 18th century glass manufacturers seeking a permanent site for their glassworks tended to build near rivers since this made it easier to transport the timber needed for fuel. The 'Renaut et Compagnie' glassworks was built at the foot of the Vosges mountains, on the Meurthe's heavily forested right bank. It faced Baccarat, the largest market town in the area, so that it had an immediate source of manpower right to hand. In the spring and autumn the logs thrown into the Meurthe and its tributaries upstream were removed and set out to dry on the riverbank near the factory, where they were then stacked. Not only was the floating of timber an economical means of transportation, it also cleansed the wood of metallic and earth salts which hindered burning. In addition, the river provided the hydraulic power necessary for the cutting workshop opened in 1810.

6. The front of the château. The central section was built when the glassworks was founded in 1764, and the two wings were added in 1840. Formerly the residence of the administrator, the château received such famous visitors as King Charles X in 1828, Marshal Canrobert in 1870, Generals Pershing, Mangin and Leclerc during the Second World War, and Prince Naruhito of Japan in 1984.

8. One of the glassworkers' houses in the factory grounds. In the 18th century glassworks factories were often built to a common plan, which included the various workshops, the château and the glassworkers' lodgings, all enclosed within a perimeter wall. From the beginning housing for seventy glassworkers and their families was available in the factory grounds. Since the length of time needed for fusion and refining was extremely variable, a bell rang at all hours of the day or night to call the glassmakers to work. The lodgings were rebuilt at the end of the 19th century. Today, although the work schedule is perfectly regular, many workers still prefer to live in the factory grounds.

10. Western façade of the main hot workshop, one of four at Baccarat, built in 1881. The original brick chimney is still in place, as is the bell which summoned the men to work. In the foreground, lime trees and acacias overlook the courtyard.

11. Close-up of the façade of the main hot workshop: between two stained-glass windows, the coat of arms of the town of Baccarat. The date 1765 corresponds to the beginning of the glassworks' activities.

12. Wagons filled with crystal composition ready for transportation to the pot furnace. Consisting essentially of sand, potassium, minium and cullet, the composition, placed in each of the twenty-one pots of the furnace, becomes, when heated, the vitreous matter 'gathered' by the glassmakers. The ultra-modern tank furnaces have not by any means completely replaced the pot furnace, which has a number of complementary uses. It provides glassmakers, for example, with a great quantity of crystal that can be diversified in as many ways as there are pots, which makes it particularly useful for the preparation of coloured crystal.

13. Work area near a tank furnace. Derived from optical furnaces, tank furnaces have electro-melting refractories and outlet tubes in platino-rhodium. Introduced in 1966, these improvements protect the crystal from possible contact with impurities, in contrast with traditional furnaces where the clay of the pots occasionally melts into the molten crystal. The tank furnace functions continuously, requiring teams of glassworkers to work in relays day and night.

14. Crystal heated to an extremely high temperature (1,050°C, c. 1,920°F) being poured into a mould. On the right, a pair of shears ready to trim off the surplus once the mould has been filled.

15. Each pot of a traditional furnace requires a team of three to six glassworkers. The gatherer's job is to remove from the pot the precise quantity of crystal required by the other members of his team.

16. A glass-blower forming a 'parison' of molten glass before blowing it into a mould.

17. At the end of a blowpipe, a 'parison' destined to become the branch of a chandelier.

18. The blowpipe, the 'ferret' and the pump are all used to remove crystal from the pot. The blowpipe is used to gather the quantity of crystal needed to blow a bowl, while the 'ferret' serves to remove smaller quantities, for the stem or foot of a glass, for example. Crystal removed by means of a pump is of better quality than that taken off with the blowpipe or 'ferret' because the pump removes crystal from below the surface, thus avoiding the impurities caused by melting in pot furnaces. Here we see the discharge mould of a pump, filled with extremely hot crystal.

19. The heat protection at the upper end of this blowpipe indicates that the glass-blower is shaping a very large bowl in a mould placed at floor level.

20. Modelling of a chandelier branch. Two workers are required to draw, twist and, in an absolutely synchronized movement, place the crystal in the mould.

Page 21. A head glassmaker at work.

22. Modelling a bowl at the end of a blowpipe.

23. The second blower places and models the foot, centring it around the stem.

24. The first blower is the team's most experienced glassworker. He has the most delicate task of all – that of placing and forming the stem on the bowl.

25. Fixing a stem on to the bowl of a vase. When it is removed from the furnace, the temperature of the crystal drops, and it changes in colour from yellow to red. As it cools, it gradually grows lighter in colour, finally becoming transparent.

26. Gilding: decorating a PRESTIGE beer mug by means of a brush dipped in a gold-based solution. The gilt is applied to motifs which have been etched into the crystal. After annealing, the gold remaining on the crystal is burnished with an agate stone to obtain a smooth and shiny finish.

27. Moulds. Since its beginnings, thousands of moulds have been produced at Baccarat. The moulds we see here have been temporarily stacked behind the hot workshop, ready for cleaning, classifying and storing in the moulds room. They remain as a kind of souvenir of the factory's production, and some of them will be re-used.

28. Sandstone and Carborundum wheels for the cutting machines. Crystal has always been cut, because the lead it contains reduces its hardness and makes it shinier than ordinary glass, and such cutting produces interesting optical effects. Over the years crystal-cutters have developed a vast variety of motifs which show off the different properties of crystal according to the depth and angle of the cut. This is why it is important to maintain a collection of wheels of varying hardness and shapes.

29. Cutting a TSAR glass. Such 'rich' cuts are made with diamond or sandstone wheels. This work is done by the most talented glass-cutters, who have received the national certification of 'Best Workman in France'.

30. Flat cuts on the bowl of a DÉSIRÉ vase.

31. Wheel-engraving: the corundum wheel, cooled by a continual trickle of water, being used to cut a hock glass from the VALLÉE service. Wheel-engravers, glassmakers, glass-cutters and bronzeworkers, like all other manual workers, can compete for the national title of 'Best Workman in France'.

32. Working with tongs on hot crystal during the preparation of a bowl in cased crystal (having a double layer of crystal, one clear, one coloured).

33. Detail of a window in Baccarat church. Built in 1953, the church is decorated with a series of stained-glass windows designed by the painters Idoux, Stahly, Poncet, Martin and Delahaye. More than fifty colours of crystal were melted to create the stained-glass slabs depicting the Stations of the Cross and the Twelve Apostles.

34. The etching process involves printing a motif on paper. The motif is the reserved pattern surrounded by an inked background. Here, the printed paper is pressed against the sides of a MICHELANGELO vase. The vase is then steeped in a vapour bath, which removes the paper while leaving the ink impression and reserved motif.

35. After it has been steeped in a vapour bath, the entire glass, with the exception of the reserved decorative motifs which are to be attacked by the acid bath, is coated with ink by a hand-finisher (usually a woman).

36. PRESTIGE wine glasses and PARME water glasses and tumblers ready for immersion in an acid bath.

37. Strict inspections occur at all stages of production. Here, a piece leaving the hot workshop on its way to the cold workshops.

38. A book containing workshop designs, a sample of one of the 19,000 models patented by Baccarat since 1861.

39. A collection of periodicals and art books in the crystalworks archives in Meurthe-et-Moselle.

40. Sales catalogues and an index of Baccarat models.

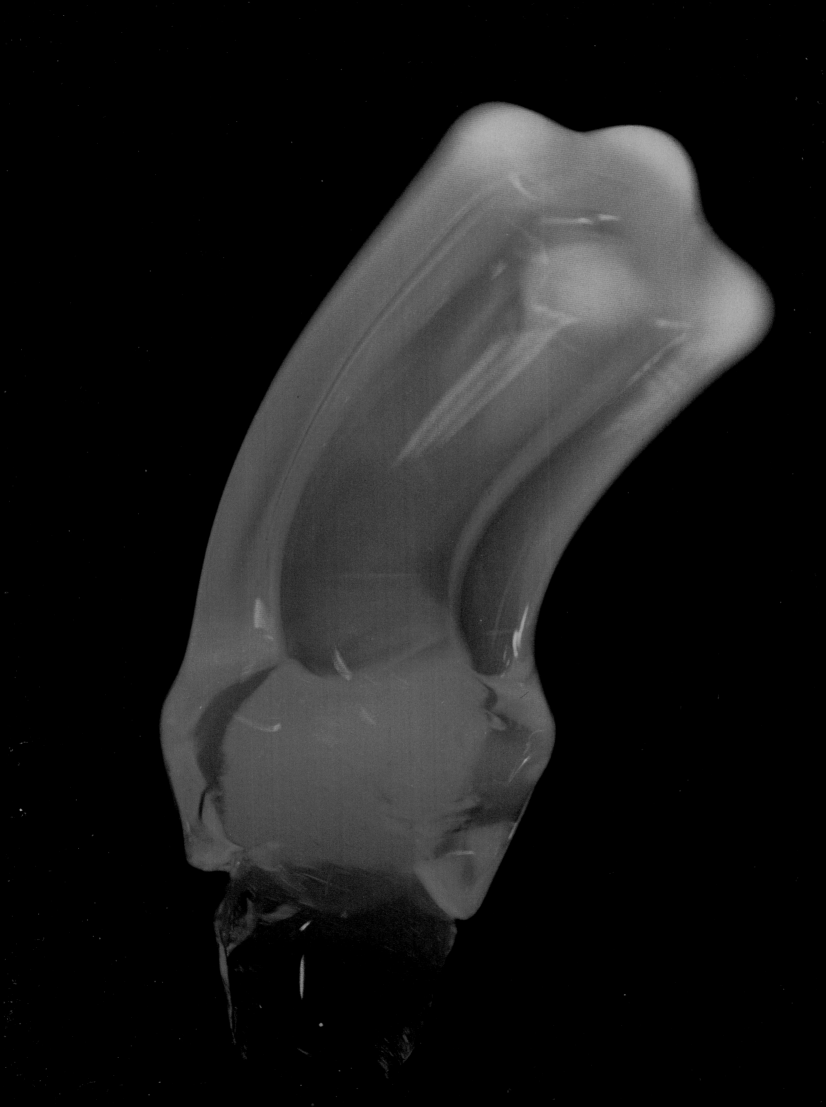

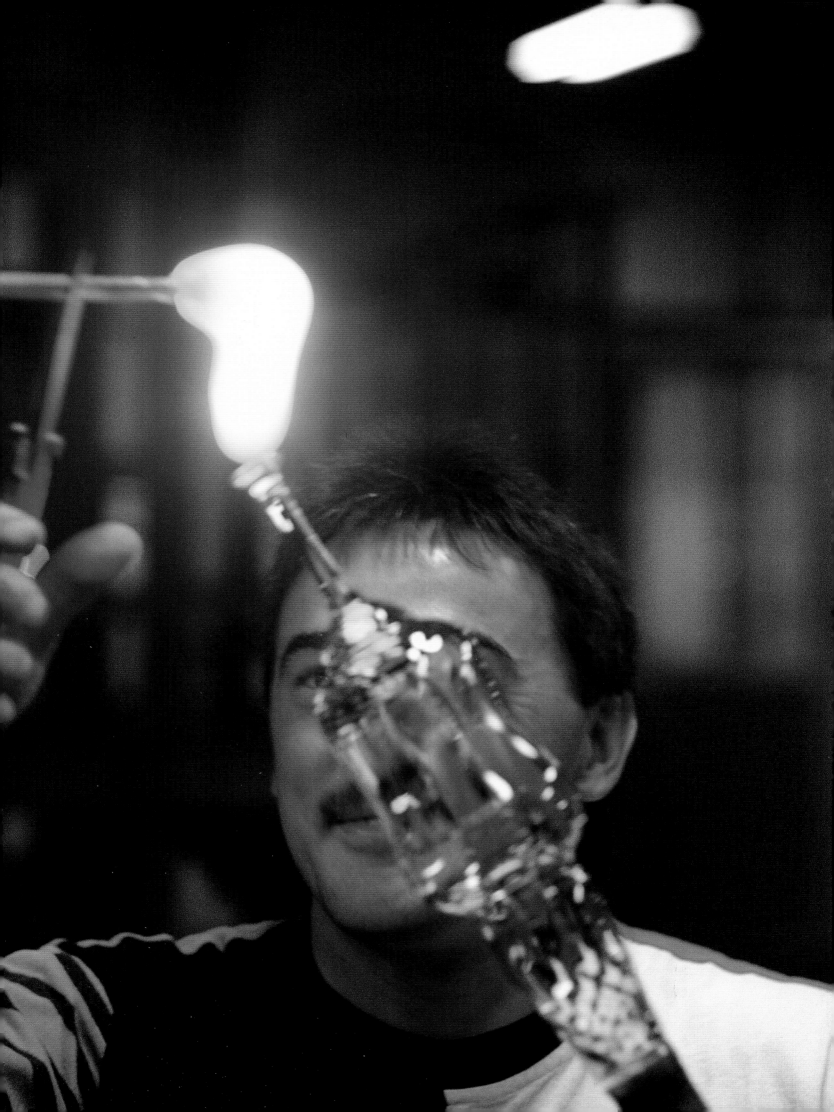

THE STORY OF BACCARAT

Jean-Louis Curtis

We tend to take for granted the various materials, products and scientific techniques that make up the essential fabric of our daily lives; it rarely occurs to us to wonder where these materials came from or how the techniques were discovered. If all glass products suddenly disappeared off the face of the earth, we would have no electric light, no windows, no glasses to drink from, no spectacles – and at least a quarter of the world's population depends on them – and no thermometers. Hospitals would be desperately short of vital equipment; laboratory work would be brought to a complete standstill; and many industries would simply cease to exist. In short, the disappearance of glass would be a universal catastrophe, paralysing many of the systems upon which we unthinkingly depend. Lighting our surroundings, closing the windows to shut out the cold, lowering or raising our car windows, wearing spectacles to correct weak vision – these are all things we take for granted, without ever stopping to wonder how this invaluable substance, glass, came into our lives.

Glass has existed since earliest antiquity, although we do not know the exact date of its first appearance, or how it was first discovered or produced, or by whom. This uncertainty has given rise to various legends during the course of time. Pliny the Elder, for example, tells us how Phoenician sailors, cooking their meal on the beach by hanging a pot over a wood fire, noticed that where the surrounding sand was licked by the flames it began to take on a glassy appearance and consistency. A good story, perhaps, but unfortunately not a very convincing one. To melt silica requires much higher temperatures (at least 1,300°C or about 2,400°F) than a campfire could produce. It is quite likely, however, that glass was discovered by accident, possibly when craftsmen were working with some other raw material, such as clay. Clay, which had from the earliest times been used to make domestic utensils, can sometimes contain silica. It would undoubtedly have taken a series of such accidents, spread over several hundred years, before potters and other craftsmen finally came to realize that an entirely new product could be created out of fine grains of sand. This realization would undoubtedly have paved the way for further experiments, again spread over a considerable period of time.

And yet artifacts exist, some of them intact, to prove that glassmaking was practised in the Near East and in Egypt between 2000 and 1500 BC. Naturally, glass was not always exactly as we know it today. The first glass was made of sand, limestone and mother of pearl, in other words crushed seashells, whereas today's material is much richer in components, comprising, in addition to silica, sodium oxide and potassium oxide (as soda and potash), plus aluminium, lime and magnesium. What the ancient Egyptians produced was a substance that was still opaque and not completely vitreous, but different from anything previously known in pottery or ceramics. Archaeologists have found Egyptian beads dating from the Sixth Dynasty, while the first small glass containers – for ointments and cosmetics – appeared in the Eighteenth Dynasty. What is particularly striking is that glass was initially used to make luxury items such as jewelry and perfume bottles rather than domestic utensils such as dishes and drinking vessels. The fact that at this date feminine accessories took priority over utilitarian objects may be a further argument in favour of regarding the first civilizations as matriarchal.

From the sixth century BC glassmaking spread through the regions of the eastern Mediterranean and the Aegean, southern Italy and Sicily. In the third century, following the conquests of Alexander the Great, the Ptolemaic capital Alexandria became an important glassmaking centre and the major manufacturer of a type of decorative glassware that has remained popular to this day – millefiori. The millefiori technique involves fusing together a number of fine coloured glass rods and then cutting through the glass crosswise to create a multicoloured mosaic resembling a dense cluster of flowers. Today paperweights and sulphides (cameos embedded in crystal) are still produced using the millefiori method.

The discovery of a new technique during the first century BC was to revolutionize the glassmaking process. This was the use of hollow pipes as a means of blowing the glass. Up until then craftsmen had pounded the molten material into a mould with a mallet or a pestle to produce simple open-shaped objects, such as bowls or cups; but they had been unable to create more complex shapes, rounded narrow-necked containers such as jars, for example. Now, however, some humble genius, whose name has long been forgotten, hit upon the idea of shaping the 'metal' (as molten glass is known) by blowing into it through a hollow tube. Glass blown by this method could be introduced into any number of different-shaped moulds.

This discovery led to the remarkable expansion of glass manufacture, resulting in genuine mass production. Now, as its application was extended from feminine accessories and luxury items, such as beads, jewelry and cosmetic containers, to household goods – cooking and eating utensils, lamps and interior decoration – glass gradually became a part of the very fabric of everyday life. It was widely used under the Roman Empire (as discoveries at Pompeii, destroyed in AD 79, amply confirm), enjoying a heyday that has only been surpassed in modern times.

The Roman conquests of Western Europe facilitated the spread of glass, first along the Rhone and Rhine valleys and later throughout Gaul. Glass funerary vases have been discovered in Frankish and Merovingian tombs, and window glass already existed during Gregory of Tours's lifetime (sixth century AD), when it was used in churches, cloisters and administrative buildings. The increasing importance of glass as early as the fourth century is clear from a decree promulgated by the Byzantine emperor granting glass craftsmen exemptions on all personal taxes – a way of recognizing not just their usefulness to the empire, but also the importance of their profession: no longer regarded as simple artisans, they were now honoured as artists. Much later, after the capture of Byzantium by the Crusaders in 1204, Venice began importing Byzantine glassmaking techniques and localizing production on Murano. The island became in fact a quasi-prison for the glassmakers since the Serenissima was determined to maintain the monopoly on the industry and to prevent the secrets of glass manufacture or glassmaking materials being smuggled out to neighbouring countries. Severe restrictions were imposed and any worker caught in breach of the regulations received heavy penalties. Murano is still famous for its exquisite glassmaking and attracts hundreds of tourists every day, but in the thirteenth century the island was out of bounds to travellers. Such protective measures ultimately proved useless, however: there was no way of isolating the new techniques and soon glassworks appeared in other Italian cities and even beyond the country's borders, in France, Germany and Flanders.

The first Venetian products to appear on the markets of Europe,

Africa and the Orient were primarily small items of glassware such as had been produced in ancient Egypt, with the accent on the frivolous rather than the functional. These were followed by glasses, goblets, jugs and dishes. Murano produced an almost colourless glass known as *cristallo* – an allusion to rock crystal – although it was not quite crystal as we know it. Venetian glassware was very ornate, fanciful and often extravagant in design, and it was enormously popular. Despite the strict surveillance imposed on their activities by the Republic of Rome, Murano glassmakers had begun emigrating abroad and the 'Venetian style' was imitated as far afield as Lyons, Rouen, Brussels and Cologne.

In the fourteenth century Germany began to market a type of Rhine wine (or hock) glass decorated with cabochons and known as a *Römer*, which became very popular. But it was in Nuremberg and Prague that so-called Bohemian glassware was developed. This new glassware began to supplant Venetian products, probably because of its more marked local or regional character, and also because the glass, being thicker, could be cut and engraved to a greater depth. Bohemian glassmakers, like the *cristallo* craftsmen, were aiming above all to produce a glass that had the luminosity of rock crystal. Rock crystal could be ground and added to the other ingredients in the composition, but the end product, when it came out of the furnace, was never quite identical to the crystal itself. It was not until the seventeenth century, in England, that the problem was finally resolved. The invention of glass-blowing had revolutionized the whole process of glassmaking towards the end of the pre-Christian era; now, seventeen hundred years later, thanks to this second discovery, glassmaking was to undergo another major transformation and produce a glass of particular brilliance – crystal.

Like many other discoveries, this one was born of necessity. Glass furnaces were naturally stoked with wood, and forests were ruthlessly plundered to supply it. In 1615 the English parliament became uneasy about the threat this posed to the country's natural woodland. If trees must be felled, parliamentarians argued, let them be felled for a cause that was vital to the security and glory of the nation, in other words, shipbuilding: maintaining the British navy was more important than manufacturing drinking vessels and vases. A law was therefore passed in 1615 prohibiting the use of wood in glass furnaces. The wood was replaced by coal, but it was soon found that the coal blackened the molten glass inside the crucibles. When the crucibles were covered to prevent this from happening, on the other hand, the inner temperature dropped too low. One possible solution was to keep the crucibles covered to prevent discolouration while at the same time reducing the melting point of the glass. In 1676 a London glassmaker by the name of George Ravenscroft, appointed by the Worshipful Company of Glass Sellers to experiment with naturally occurring materials, hit on the idea of using lead oxide as a flux or facilitator in the melting process.

The result was a glass of much greater density than any produced before, but one that had other, even more important, qualities – brilliancy and luminosity – and, what was more, produced, when lightly struck, a long-drawn-out, 'crystalline' sound. George Ravenscroft had discovered lead crystal. He had merely stumbled upon his discovery while looking for ways to reduce the inconveniences of coal heating, but his technique would be perfected over the next few decades and adopted by numerous continental glassworks.

Our investigation now takes us forward a century to 1764, and across to Lorraine in eastern France. Under the *ancien régime* in

France, in addition to spiritual authority, the higher clergy enjoyed certain temporal powers based on landownership. One such important landowner was the Bishop of Metz, His Grace Louis de Montmorency-Laval, whose vast estates included the *châtellenie* of Baccarat. (A *châtellenie* under the *ancien régime* was the totality of land under the jurisdiction of a *châtelain*.) The soil at Baccarat was not particularly suitable for growing wheat due to its high levels of silica. The land was heavily wooded, however, and the bishop, eager to make the best possible use of its natural resources, decided that it offered a perfect site for a wood-burning factory. In 1764 he therefore sent a petition to Louis XV (since to set up any industry required royal authorization), in which he put forward various patriotic and humanitarian arguments in support of his request: 'Sire, it is on account of the fact that France produces no artistic glassware of her own that Bohemian products enter our country in such great numbers; hence, the astonishingly large exportation of deniers, and this at a time, precisely, when the kingdom has a great need of them in order to speed its recovery from the ravages of the Seven Years' War [1756–63], and when our woodcutters are without work, as they have been since 1760.'

The king approved the bishop's request at Fontainebleau on 16 October 1764 and four months later, on 16 February 1765, signed the letters patent, which were registered by the parliament of Metz.

The bishop's first practical concern was to devise a method of transporting wood from the forest to the furnaces. Clearly, the simplest and cheapest way was to float the logs down by river. With this in mind, he looked for a site as close as possible to the River Meurthe, eventually deciding on Baccarat. The town, on the left bank, provided an immediate source of manpower, while a large

The name Baccarat may possibly derive from the Latin *Bacchi ara*, 'altar of Bacchus' (the Roman god of wine), the remains of such an altar having apparently been found near a Roman settlement in the vicinity of Baccarat.

A baccarat has come, by extension, to mean 'a piece of crystalware manufactured at Baccarat'.

area of open land on the right bank offered a suitable site for the factory itself. (The Baccarat crystalworks is still standing today on the original site.)

On 12 June 1776 the bishop formed a partnership with Antoine Renaut, a highly qualified glassmaker, and Léopold, Seigneur de Corny. Renaut bought a third share in the glassworks, and de Corny, whose estates lay near Metz, provided the financial backing for the business.

Accommodation for seventy workers and their families was built in the factory grounds. For various technical reasons, the time it took for glass to melt tended to vary in those days, and the melting point could be reached at any moment of the day or night. It was imperative that the workers be housed close by the factory so that, when the melting process began, they could be summoned to their stations by a bell. From the start, therefore, Baccarat was a self-contained community, and this sense of community continues to be a feature of the firm today.

During its first twenty years the glassworks appears to have prospered, to judge from accounts relating to consumption of wood and sand. Then came the Revolution and the First Empire with its endless wars – years so difficult that, in December 1806, the business had to be sold at auction. It was bought by a merchant from Nancy. But the nation lay in economic ruins, the price of fuel had risen to exorbitant levels, the British blockade had imposed a stranglehold on French industry, and of the glassworks' four hundred workers three hundred and thirty had to be dismissed.

Business recovered gradually after the fall of Napoleon. It was then that the glassworks switched to manufacturing crystal. In 1816 it was sold again, this time to Aimé-Gabriel d'Artigues, owner of a crystal factory in the Belgian town of Vonêche. Following the treaty of 1815 customs duties were so high that it no longer paid to export goods from Belgium to France, so d'Artigues sent a petition to Louis XVIII requesting exemption from such duties. The king agreed, on condition that d'Artigues set up a crystalworks in France. Louis could only have applauded his own decision when he visited the Exposition Nationale in Paris in 1823 and saw the dazzling array of objects from the Baccarat workshop.

'Perfection' was, and continued to be, the key word of the new firm. It was sold again in 1823, and one of the three new owners, Pierre-Antoine Godard-Desmarest, was particularly exacting with regard to the quality of its products – standards of perfection he succeeded in instilling in both his partners and his workforce. This attention to quality encompassed both raw materials (which included fine-grain sand and potassium imported from America) and workmanship, and all Baccarat glassworkers underwent a lengthy and meticulous training. The perfectionist tradition has continued and accounts for the highly individualized quality of Baccarat glassware and its worldwide reputation today.

During the century and a half since the foundation of the crystalworks a series of technical innovations has led to improvements in working conditions, increased output, and products of increasingly high quality. It was in the heating procedures that the most spectacular advances were made. Towards the middle of the nineteenth century, sweeping industrialization throughout France led to the construction of many new factories in Lorraine, in particular china and tile factories, ironworks and breweries. Wood, once so abundant that the Bishop of Metz had merely been anxious to find a way of exploiting it, was becoming scarce, and there was now a real need to find new sources of fuel. Coal gas turned out to be too expensive. Then, in 1867, the Siemens furnace made its appearance. Operating on wood gas, it made for savings in fuel, but was also responsible for a reduction in the volume of the heated material, so that 144 pounds of raw material would only produce 100 pounds of marketable crystal. In order to reduce the variations in melting time, the wood was first dried and cut into logs of equal size, then fed into the furnaces at regular intervals. In this way a constant temperature could be maintained and the melting point be predicted with greater accuracy. In 1867 another German engineer by the name of Boetius invented a furnace whose value lay in requiring the participation of only a section of the workforce. This particular type of furnace remained in use for fifty years. Coal as a fuel made its debut in 1871 and continued to be used until 1932, when it was replaced by coal gas generators. Today Baccarat uses natural gas from the Commonwealth of Independent States.

In 1824 a glassmaker called Ismaïl Robinet invented a pump (which still bears his name today) designed for blowing simple pieces that did not require the specialized skills of a qualified glassmaker. Then, in 1838, Baccarat offered a prize of thirty thousand francs to the first technician to discover a method of producing coloured glass, so rivalling Bohemian production. The prize was won – and with it the position of assistant director – by François-Eugène de Fontenay, and Baccarat's coloured glassware became as popular as millefiori.

These developments were all in the area of what is known as 'hot work', that part of the glassmaking process concerned with the molten 'metal'. Other developments directly affected the so-called 'cold work' processes. Up until 1810/11 cutters used a foot pedal to activate a belt-driven wheel on which they cut the crystal. This day-long pedalling was obviously exhausting and a cutting machine with hydraulically operated lapidary's wheels was designed to replace the foot pedal. Like Robinet's pump, this new invention had a twofold advantage: while reducing physical effort, it also increased production.

It was this constant search for technical innovations and improvements that made Baccarat the firm it is today. These material developments were matched, almost from the start, by a series of measures reflecting an extraordinarily progressive attitude to workers' rights. In addition to housing, Baccarat workers have had access to free medical assistance since 1827, an insurance scheme since 1835, and, since 1851, a pension fund for the glass-cutters, engravers and gilders, extended eight years later to include the rest of the workforce. In 1821 the company opened a savings bank with general interest rates of five per cent, at a time when the interest rate at most other banks was less than four per cent. Education of apprentices was another of its concerns and in 1827 it opened a boarding school for two hundred children. In 1890 it created a fund for the unemployed.

All these measures were adopted at a time when French workers generally were in a painfully precarious position, deprived of any benefits that might have protected them against illness, unemployment and old age. Such benefits were only instituted in the first third of the twentieth century. In 1930, at the request of the Secretary of State, André Tardieu, Pierre Laval set up a national insurance scheme, while the forty-hour week and paid holidays were put into effect by the Popular Front.

Baccarat was inevitably accused of 'paternalism' for its policy with regard to its workers. Clearly, such a policy was motivated in part by a concern for efficiency: the business depended on the quality of its products, and to achieve this quality required training workers to a highly skilled level and then continuing to employ them – retaining their loyalty by offering them benefits they were unable to find elsewhere. Be that as it may, many other companies in France were in a similar position but used very different methods for keeping on their workforce: rather than adopt such social reforms, they constantly fuelled their employees' fears of dismissal and subsequent unemployment and poverty. Baccarat's managers were the first to understand that the national economy was about to enter a new era characterized by a system of mutual advantage between labour and management, and that prosperity and social harmony could only be achieved at this price. It is plausible to suppose – in view of what we know of Baccarat's working procedures – that, rather than accepting these changes as a regrettable necessity, they welcomed them as a matter of fairness.

There is a certain type of thinking in France that necessarily considers all social progress in bourgeois society as a fraud, a concealed form of exploitation. Even until very recently, after the collapse of Communism and the grim realization of what seventy years of Marxist rule had done for the former Soviet Union and its people, a French journalist would still report that he had just returned from a Soviet kolkhoz and that everything was wonderful there, that everyone was blissfully happy, and that if you wanted to see deprivation and distress in the West you only had to go to the Auvergne. The accusation of paternalism laid at Baccarat's door in its early days is of a piece with this.

At the beginning of the nineteenth century, as the effects of the

Napoleonic Wars abated, Baccarat began to flourish and its reputation was consolidated by official approval from various sovereigns and heads of state. At the 1823 Exposition Nationale in Paris, it was Baccarat's crystalware which Louis XVIII particularly admired, appreciating its combination of 'beautiful workmanship' and relatively 'modest prices'. The objects of his admiration were in fact simple pieces in comparison to later products from the Baccarat workshop, notably during the Second Empire.

It was Charles X's visit to the crystalworks in 1828, however, that had the most significant repercussions for the company. The king, who had a clear sense of where industry in France was going, was determined to visit each of the workshops in turn and to observe the different phases of production. 'The prosperity of a firm and the wellbeing of a nation depend on available goods,' he said to the company's director, M. Godard-Desmarest, forecasting, more than a century in advance, the advent of the consumer society, 'and their success consists in making practical, elegant and reasonably priced goods available to the greatest number of purchasers.' The crystal-works presented the monarch with a gift of two magnificent Medici vases, a large crystal ewer, a fifteen-piece tea service and a five-piece water set. The king, in return, ordered a dinner service for the Tuileries, while the Duchesse d'Angoulême personally chose a set of eighteen glasses, described by her as 'stable, sturdy, balanced, perfect'.

Louis-Philippe and Napoleon II also visited the crystalworks and were followed by a succession of French presidents and foreign heads of state.

Under the Second Empire, a period of major commercial and industrial growth in France, the crystalworks enjoyed one of its several heydays. Napoleon III, who established the Second Empire in 1852, was not in fact the unenlightened despot official historians have made him out to be. The author of an essay entitled *Extinction du paupérisme* (Abolition of Pauperism) setting out his doctrine on social issues, he took a keen interest in economic development and in the condition of the workers. Impressed by his visit to the Great Exhibition at London's Crystal Palace in 1851, he decided that France should organize a rival event. The result was the Exposition Internationale of 1855, which attracted more than five million visitors, including Queen Victoria and Prince Albert. It was followed, in 1867, by another exhibition, the most splendid occasion of its kind so far and which boasted so many royal visitors – Tsar Alexander II, Wilhelm I of Prussia, the Emperor Franz Joseph I of Austria, Léopold II of Belgium, Ludwig II of Bavaria, the Kings of Greece, Portugal and Württemberg, the Khedive of Egypt, among them – that it prompted the Goncourts to say that it was 'raining kings'. Baccarat won a Gold Medal at the 1855 exhibition and has continued to carry off the top prizes at international exhibitions ever since. One of its exhibits in 1867, a gigantic fountain twenty-four feet tall, with a basin ten feet in diameter, simply took the visitors' breath away. At the Exposition Universelle of 1878, where the prizes were presented by Louis, the young Prince Imperial, in his first official role, Baccarat showed a pavilion housing a statue of the god Mercury, the Temple of Mercury, which stands today in a private garden just outside Barcelona. Other notable Baccarat exhibits included a pair of five-foot Medici vases.

The success of these exhibitions, the royal presence at the inauguration of the Suez Canal, and the welcome extended to the Empress Eugénie (wife of Napoleon III) in Constantinople and

A lithograph commemorating Baccarat's success at the Expositions Universelles of 1867
and 1878, published in a sales catalogue in c. 1880.

An ordinance issued by King Louis XVIII, 9–12 April 1817. Following an ordinance issued on 7 March 1816, this document gave royal authorization to Aimé-Gabriel d'Artigues to start a crystal factory in the 'Sainte-Anne Glassworks near Baccarat'. The factory was to consist of four furnaces of twelve pots each, and was to be called the 'Vonêche Glassworks at Baccarat'.

Facing page: the Temple of Mercury (height: 5 m/16 ft; diameter: 5.25 m/17 ft). Consisting of sections of cut crystal supported by an internal metallic structure, and housing a reproduction in silver-plated bronze of Giambologna's famous *Flying Mercury* (Florence, 1574), this circular, domed Greek temple was displayed at the Exposition Universelle of 1878. The critics praised Baccarat, 'which France can rightly consider as one of her national glories', for its technical brilliance, but showed little enthusiasm for the glass version of a structure traditionally made in marble. Disappointed, the crystalworks refused to exhibit at other major exhibitions held in France. Only in 1909, in Nancy, did Baccarat exhibit once more, and again in 1910 at the Musée Galliera in Paris. The Temple of Mercury was purchased in 1892 by the King of Portugal, then in 1917 relocated to a pond on a private property near Barcelona, where it has been ever since.

The warehouse, Rue de Paradis, c. 1860. As of 1831–32, the Baccarat, Saint-Louis, Bercy and Choisy crystalworks entrusted the common management of their sales to Launay, Hautin et Cie. Located on Rue de Paradis in a former relay stable, the company was managed by Jean-Baptiste Launay, a competent businessman who developed the market for crystalware throughout France and maintained the demand for a constant renewal of designs. He engaged bronzemakers and glass enamellers such as Jean-François Robert, and developed the vogue for painted crystal with gilded bronze embellishments. This commercial arrangement ended in 1857, with Baccarat and Saint-Louis sharing the real estate. In conjunction with the commercial activities of its warehouse, Baccarat now developed its own workshops devoted to designing and decorating: drawing, gilding, enamelling, bronzework and photography. These workshops did not replace the crystalworks' other workshops, but produced designs for luxury items, for which they hired their own designers, including, from 1907 to 1911, the famous glass enameller Auguste Heiligenstein. The warehouse itself became a fashionable spot for royalty and other celebrities to visit.

Facing page: 'The Baccarat Crystalworks in 1837'. Ink wash on heavy paper, signed V. Venelle, kept at the crystalworks. In the foreground, the River Meurthe and the bridge linking the town to the factory since 1775. In the centre, the crystalworks with its workshops, workers' houses, manager's château, chapel (1775) and tree-lined courtyard. In the background, the Vosges mountains.

LES CRISTALLERIES DE BACCARAT
EN 1857

Cairo, all helped to open up the Near East to Baccarat crystalware and other products of French art and industry. The Shah of Persia, the Sultan of Turkey and the Khedive of Egypt acquired huge candelabra and chandeliers of the sort that already adorned France's royal palaces and châteaux, nothing being too large or too dear for these Eastern rulers eager to transform their numerous residences into fairy palaces of light. Much later, in 1930, the prize for sheer extravagance was to go to the Maharajah of Gwalior, who built a palace expressly for the purpose of housing a certain chandelier, known as the Hall Oriental. When it was finally installed, the ceiling collapsed and the chandelier shattered. Undeterred, the maharajah built another, sturdier palace, had his heaviest elephant hoisted on to the roof by means of a crane to test its strength, then ordered another chandelier.

Baccarat made numerous chandeliers during the Second Empire, though its major product was dinner services, followed by perfume bottles, paperweights and a number of other either practical or purely decorative articles. Apparently, there was even a demand for crystal chamber pots.

The Russians also contributed to the prosperity of Baccarat in the second half of the nineteenth century, proving as extravagant in their consumption of crystalware as the sultans and maharajahs had done. Indeed, what could be more profitable than clients who bought vast quantities of merchandise, only to smash their purchases immediately after use and buy more? For this was precisely what Russian aristocrats did – drinking, then tossing the glass – even a Baccarat glass – over their shoulder and leaving the servants to sweep up the bits. It was a custom adopted by the first tsars – the idea being that no one else should drink from a glass touched by their own venerable

The end of a working day at the crystalworks, summer 1886.

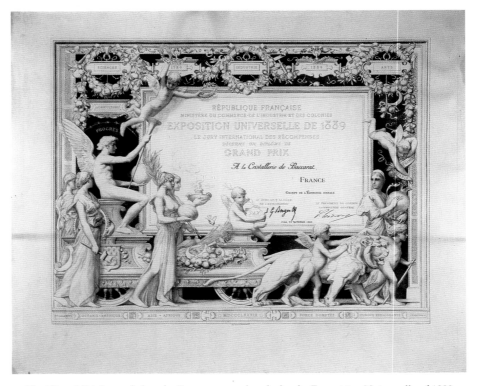

The 'Grand Prix' awarded to the Baccarat crystalworks by the Exposition Universelle of 1889.
That year Baccarat exhibited in the section entitled 'Social Economy' and presented its efforts
on behalf of its workforce: salaries, insurance and retirement schemes, credit, unemployment
benefits, schooling for boys and girls, housing, etc. These were provisions in response to,
and at times anticipating, legislation concerning the rights of workers developed during the
Third Republic.

lips – and generations of grand dukes and noblemen followed suit. At Baccarat a third of the workforce, which totalled more than two thousand, was exclusively involved in filling the orders of the Russian aristocracy. This state of affairs came to an abrupt end in 1917: the Russians' Soviet successors broke many things, but not glasses. Khrushchev was the last Communist leader to be seen breaking his glass after drinking from it during an official dinner at the Ministry of Foreign Affairs in Paris. Brezhnev did not follow his example, but when he held a luncheon for President Giscard d'Estaing at the new Soviet embassy building, Baccarat received an important order for Capri glasses. It was the last gesture of its kind the Soviet government was to make.

Baccarat had been founded a quarter of a century before the French Revolution; forty years later, under the First Empire, it almost collapsed. Like many other industries in France, like France itself, it was to endure a series of crises: the revolutions of 1830 and 1848, the Franco-Prussian War of 1870–71, and, in our own century, two World Wars. Each time it tottered on the brink of bankruptcy; each time it was saved by the intelligence of its managers, the loyalty of the workforce and the spirit of solidarity that was such a salient characteristic of the firm. The political situation in 1830 caused such widespread panic that sales dropped almost to zero. A number of furnaces were extinguished, output was reduced and workers who had invested in the business were reimbursed at great cost to the company. The cumulative losses were staggering, but Baccarat survived nevertheless. In 1848 there was a rerun of events. No workers were dismissed, but a great number were made temporarily redundant and drew half-pay.

Worse was to come during the two World Wars. In 1914 the

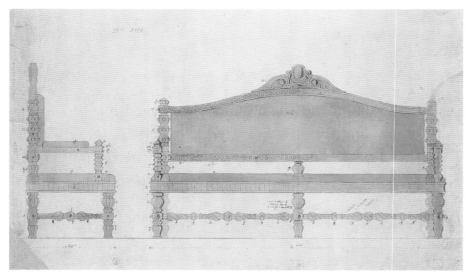

Study for a crystal canapé (length: 2 m/6 ft 7 in.) and armchair, 1885, designed to match a series of crystal chairs made in 1883. The identity of the client is unknown. The ensemble may have been designed for a maharajah, since there was a vast market for crystal furniture in India after 1876. (The Thomas Osler Company of Birmingham made it its speciality.) Baccarat began to receive commissions for furniture in 1883, and in 1886 sought to exploit this market by opening a branch in Bombay. At the same time it expanded its commercial network to include the United States, Russia, Japan, and Latin America (Mexico, Argentina, Uruguay and Brazil), as well as Asia following its participation in the 1887 Exhibition in Hanoi. Baccarat's successful turnover on the foreign market made it the number one exporter of crystal.

Facing page: design for a large armchair, ink on tracing paper, 1886. This drawing, which accompanied a commission for a crystal throne, was most probably for an Indian client.

majority of employees were called up, many never to return. The Germans invaded Baccarat on 25 August, retreating on 12 September after their defeat on the Marne. The château was used as a military hospital and throughout the war the factory remained within range of the heavy artillery. Production did not grind to a complete halt, but, instead of luxury goods, the workshops were now manufacturing miners' lamps. For safety reasons, lighting in the mines presented serious difficulties, which Baccarat helped to resolve by improving the standards of protection. On 17 June 1940 the factory was invaded once again and this time it was turned into a huge prison camp. During the Occupation some 180 workers were sent to German labour camps. When their troops finally withdrew, the Nazis endeavoured to transport the company's entire stocks of crystalware back to Germany but were prevented from doing so by the state of the railways. Following the Liberation, Baccarat gradually resumed its normal activities, as it had succeeded in doing after each previous crisis.

Since 1945 the workshops have undergone a series of major transformations. The old brick furnaces were replaced by three large tank furnaces. The first of these, completed in 1966, and the only furnace in Europe fitted with platino-rhodium tubes, produced a crystal of a particularly pure quality. The two other furnaces were built in 1976 and 1986. All the cutting workshops were re-equipped with diamond wheels and working practices were gradually stream-lined so that individual units became responsible for manufacturing their own individual product. Today the various workshops are interconnected by some two miles of concrete pathways.

Where working conditions and social benefits were concerned, Baccarat more than met its legal obligations by setting up a benefit fund, to be managed entirely by the workers themselves, and successfully introducing several shareholding schemes. Progressive company policies in this area are a long-standing tradition, and they have paid off: since its foundation, Baccarat has never once been faced with a strike.

The market for Baccarat glassware has changed since the days when Eastern potentates and Russian aristocrats snapped it up in such extravagant quantities. Its major consumers now are the world's two wealthiest nations – Japan and America. In 1948 Baccarat's current chairman, René de Chambrun, founded a New York subsidiary, whose clients have come to include such major stores as Neiman Marcus in Houston, while on permanent exhibition in the Kanemori Museum in the Japanese town of Hakodate are copies of some of Baccarat's finest pieces, including Charles X's crystal ewer, the Medici vases and the royal water set.

Baccarat has been in existence now for more than two hundred years and is the world's leading manufacturer of crystalware. One might reasonably suppose that a world-famous company of its kind would be housed in majestic surroundings, something ultra-modern, perhaps, reflecting the sky from a futurist Plexiglas and aluminium façade. Instead, what we find is a large late-twentieth-century industrial complex enclosed within eighteenth-century walls. On two sides of the rectangular, tree-lined square are rows of workers' cottages, carefully maintained but exactly as they were when they were first built. At one end of the square stands the delightful little château that once served as home to the factory's managers, and next to it a chapel; and at the other end are the factory buildings, now looking decidedly antiquated – an appearance deliberately preserved to underline the age of the company and the long-standing 'family' tradition upon which it is based. The window-boxes are full of flowers, and everything looks sparklingly clean, but in a homely and welcoming, not a clinical, way.

Before entering the factory itself visitors are given a brief introduction to crystal and the crystalmaking process. The physical properties of crystal relate to its density, its hardness, the degree to which it refracts light and the quality of the sound – that delicate, long-drawn-out note – it emits when lightly struck. The term 'crystal' can only be applied to glass which contains at least twenty-four per cent lead oxide, while crystal made with thirty per cent lead is called 'full lead' or '*crystal supérieur*'. The composition of crystal varies from one glassworks to another. At Baccarat it is made up of three parts silica, two parts lead oxide, one part potash, three parts cullet, or recycled crystal, and one part various other chemical substances. This mixture is heated in the furnaces – either pot ovens or fire-clay crucibles, or the more sophisticated tank furnaces – at a temperature of approximately 1,500°C (2,700°F) until it becomes a white-hot molten mass ready for blowing.

On first entering the factory's hot workshop, the visitor is struck by the almost surreal beauty of the place. Here, in this cavernous chamber, among the blazing mouths of the furnaces, among the wooden benches and the wells sunk into the floor, workmen weave in and out according to laws that are apparently immutable but defy comprehension by the casual observer. Several of these men carry long metal tubes, on the end of which is balanced, fresh from the furnace, a quivering incandescent ball of 'metal', sticky and reddish-coloured – the crystal itself. And, although they brush past one another with every step, the extraordinary fact remains that no one ever seems to get burnt, for each of these fire-carriers follows his own

Design for a bowl, c. 1866. Ink wash, watercolour and gouache on heavy paper. The drawing was used by Jean-Baptiste Simon as the model for the wheel-engraving of a design on a large serving dish in crimson-cased crystal, shown with a pair of allegorical vases (pages 238–41) at the Exposition Universelle of 1867.

predetermined route. The whole operation is like a corps de ballet, with each individual dancer executing his own set of figures. The 'ballet' unfolds against the background roar of the furnaces (which must be kept constantly alight), a single note interrupted only by the odd word or phrase in the glassmakers' own special coded language.

The visitor, feeling almost like an intruder in some grave ceremonial rite, moves forward cautiously, anxious to avoid the incandescent globes dancing around like giant fireflies; but there is no real danger: the workmen know their job too well. And thanks to the guide's explanations the various operations gradually begin to make sense. The crystalmaking process is divided into two major stages: the hot work (rough shaping, blowing and moulding), which takes place here, in the hot workshop, and the cold work (cutting, engraving and polishing), carried out in the other workshops.

Each glassmaker has a specific function and each function, like each tool and each phase of the glassmaking process, has a traditional name (one that it has had for over two hundred years). The glassmakers are known collectively as the Chair or Shop and the glassmaking hierarchy comprises a *premier souffleur* (gaffer or first blower), a *second souffleur* (second blower), a *carreur* (shaper), a *cueilleur* (gatherer) and a *grand gamin no. 1* and *grand gamin no. 2* (first and second boy). Each member of this team of six performs a role that is vital and complementary to those of the others. In the early days of glassmaking the term 'boys' would almost certainly have been applied to young glassmakers who had completed their apprenticeship; today, depending on professional qualifications and personal preference, a glassmaker can remain a 'boy' right up until retirement age.

The process of manufacturing a crystal glass is as follows. With his blowpipe, which he has first heated in the furnace, the gatherer collects a ball of 'metal', now a beautiful orange colour due to the high temperature to which it has been exposed. By delicately and continuously rotating the blowpipe between his fingers he ensures that the incandescent material retains its symmetrical shape. Holding the blowpipe horizontally, the gatherer then carries it to the shaper, who pre-shapes the 'metal' with a wooden paddle resembling an oblong ladle, preparatory to blowing and moulding it. Holding the blowpipe vertically now and continuing to rotate it gently, the shaper blows through the mouthpiece to form a bowl, or bubble of molten glass, in the mould.

This is where the second phase of the operation begins. The blowpipe (still being rotated continuously) is passed to the gaffer at the chair and rested on the sloping arms of the chair. Using a solid metal rod known as a 'ferret', the second boy gathers from the pot a small oval mass of crystal, intended for the stem of the glass, and presents it to the gaffer. Now comes the most fascinating part of the whole hot work cycle, and the part demanding the greatest skill. The gaffer draws out the oval mass to the required length and thickness, taking great care not to overstretch it – a process sometimes achieved with the help of compasses, but more often than not simply with the naked eye. Everything happens so fast that, at more or less the same

The warehouse, Rue de Paradis, c. 1898. The abundance of chandeliers exhibited in the central
section of the store is a reminder of Baccarat's determination to compete with the English
chandelier industry. At the Exposition Nationale of 1827, Baccarat was the only French
crystalworks to show individual chandelier parts. In 1840 it became the first factory in France to
manufacture chandeliers and candelabra, exhibiting a pair of giant candelabra (height: 5.25 m/17 ft;
with 90 candles) at the Exposition Universelle of 1855. Electrification began in 1888, leading to the
modification of existing models and the creation of new ones.

moment, the first boy is fetching a ball of molten crystal from the furnace with his 'ferret' and handing it to the second blower, who uses a pair of shears to snip off the precise amount required to make the base of the glass, which he continues to rotate on a rolling plate. Once the gaffer and the second blower have done their work, the glass (still glowing) is carried mechanically to the tunnel-shaped annealing oven, or lehr, through which it passes on a conveyor belt. It remains in the lehr for roughly two and a half hours, being gradually reheated and then uniformly cooled. Only when completely cold is the glass ready for cutting.

Another important part of the hot work is the manufacture of coloured glass. The process, discovered in 1838 by François-Eugène de Fontenay (looking for a way to compete with Bohemian glass manufacturers, as we saw earlier), has obviously been greatly improved since. The colour is produced by adding metals or metallic oxides to the basic mixture: cobalt oxide, for example, produces blue; nickel oxide, purple; uranium oxide, yellow; while red and orange are produced by the addition, respectively, of gold and silver. To produce multicoloured effects, layers of molten crystal are superimposed in different colours and the crystal is later cut at different depths to reveal the various colours according to the required pattern.

Before moving on to the cold workshop, the glass, now thoroughly cooled, is examined to ensure that it has the correct dimensions and is absolutely blemish-free. This part of the operation is done by women, known as *choisisseuses* (selectors), in a special workshop of their own. These women are trained to spot the slightest imperfection – a stem that is a fraction of a millimetre longer or thicker than specified, a base that is a fraction of a millimetre wider, the minutest air bubble trapped in the crystal, a scratch invisible to the untrained eye. Any glass found to have a fault, however small, is discarded and sent for recycling; broken pieces, or cullet, from such rejects are then used in another batch.

Those items that pass the test are now ready for the cutter. But first the glass must be 'cracked off'; in other words, the 'cap' of excess glass that connected the blowpipe to the ball of molten crystal must be removed. The cut-line is scored with a diamond wheel, then exposed to a sudden blast of heat, which causes the 'cap' to break off. The rough edge is then smoothed with diamond grinding wheels and reheated to be given a final polish.

The cutters' workshop is strikingly peaceful after the roar of the hot workshop furnaces. Like the hot work processes, the glass-cutter's job is highly skilled, requiring aesthetic judgment coupled with supreme dexterity and absolute precision – qualities, in other words, proper to the artist. An impressive number of Baccarat cutters have won the title of 'Best Workman in France', the highest distinction to which any craftsman can aspire, equivalent to the artists' and sculptors' Prix de Rome. The cutter's art consists of cutting the crystal at minutely varying depths to produce the required motifs or designs. To do this he uses a variety of small wheels made of Carborundum (silicon carbide), sandstone or diamond rotating at extremely high speed and each able to cut to a different depth. Instead of applying the wheel to the crystal, the cutter delicately moves the glass against the wheel – as if he were an artist moving his canvas beneath a fixed brush, or his paper beneath a pencil, rather than the other way around.

There are several types of cut depending on the complexity of the design. 'Flat cuts' were used in 1841 for Baccarat's classic Harcourt

0,75

Studies for serving bowls on stems, c. 1850. Pencil drawing with gouache and watercolour.

Facing page: study for a pedestal table, 1861. Pencil drawing with gouache and watercolour on heavy paper. The proposed size of this item (height: 72 cm/2 ft 4 in.; diameter: 75 cm/2 ft 5 in.) makes it more a piece of furniture than an article for the table. The fashion for glass furniture was developed by Marie-Jeanne-Rosalie Désarnaud-Charpentier, director of the Escalier de Cristal ('Crystal Staircase'), a shop opened near the Palais-Royal in Paris in 1802. The shop had its own design workshops – directed by the painter Nicolas-Henri Jacob – and decorating workshops for glass-cutting and bronzework. Its crystal was supplied by the Vonêche crystalworks, and probably after 1816 by Baccarat itself. After 1851 the Expositions Universelles encouraged a veritable rivalry between Baccarat and the English company F. & C. Osler in the production of monumental objects made of crystal – fountains, candelabra, temples and extravagant pieces of furniture.

service, the table service favoured by royalty and heads of state and in crystalware what the Rolls-Royce is to the motor industry or Chanel to *haute couture*. While the essence of the flat cut is simplicity and purity, 'rich cuts', as their name suggests, involve rich and elaborate detail. The Colbert service is an example of this type of cutting. The Renaissance service uses 'hollow cuts' and the highly ornamental Prestige service with its lavish gold decoration is the service that has traditionally tended to find its way into the palaces of sultans and maharajahs.

Cutting is followed by engraving, and in some cases gilding. Wheel-engraving is a practice that has been in use for many years. While straightforward cutting can produce regular geometric patterns, wheel-engraving uses a minute lapidary's wheel to cut elaborate designs such as flowers, figures and monograms deep into the crystal. Another engraving technique widely used today is that of etching. A stencil of the design is applied to the glass and the rest of the glass is coated with resistant ink known as Judaean bitumen; the glass is then immersed in a bath of hydrofluoric acid, which attacks the unprotected areas of the crystal. Gilding, another extraordinarily delicate task (and one done by women at Baccarat), involves the application of narrow threads of gold using a very fine brush.

A visit to either of Baccarat's two museums – in the château at Baccarat itself or in Rue de Paradis, adjoining the showrooms – reveals how styles have changed over the last two hundred years. Architecture, interior design and furnishings, clothing, domestic appliances, goldwork and the plastic arts all reflect these changing trends. Yet throughout successive developments Baccarat has never been ruled by fashion or deviated from strict principles of moderation and restraint. Baccarat crystalware has remained in essence classical, even avoiding the excesses of the Second Empire, when the vogue for ornament spilled over into ostentation. For all their lavish magnificence, even Baccarat's gigantic chandeliers and candelabra dating from those years have a natural elegance and restraint.

The first table services created at Baccarat had very simple shapes. More elaborate designs were introduced at the end of the 1830s under the influence of Romanticism, with medieval and Renaissance art serving as inspiration. It was at around this time that coloured glass made its appearance, together with a semi-transparent type of glass imitating porcelain. Opal crystal (today a rare collector's item) was popular during the reign of Louis-Philippe (1830–48), while between 1870 and 1900 there was a fashion for deep cuts and engravings, and also for those beautiful coloured vases decorated with floral motifs that were to be scorned thirty years later, and which fetch huge sums in auction rooms today. Extraordinary changes in style were to follow the Great War. Women suddenly began to wear short, tomboyish hairstyles and shapeless knee-length shifts. Interior decoration, furnishings and goldwork all underwent a similar kind of reductionism. The Exposition des Arts Décoratifs of 1925 revealed to an astonished public an almost puritanical quest for spareness and simplicity. The trend naturally extended to crystalware too. Georges Chevalier, one of the great names to be associated with Baccarat, continued to produce figurative work – in particular his magnificent animal sculptures – but with a tendency towards stylization.

Such stylization has become a regular feature of Baccarat designs, whether emanating from their own design workshop or created by well-known artists for Baccarat. Certain strikingly simple pieces

Study for a monumental Medici vase on a stand, for the Exposition Universelle of 1855 or 1867.
Pencil drawing and ink wash on heavy paper.

Medici vase shown in several different sizes at the Exposition in Nancy in 1909. Scrolls, laurel leaves and gadroons have been cut into the crystal; moulded pagan mask-like faces and lion claws have been chased on the gilded bronze support.

have the quality of abstract art: Emilio Giglioli's *Château fort* (Fortress), for example, or Robert Rigot's *Terre et Cosmos* (Earth and Cosmos), Thomas Bastide's *La Liberté à l'infini* (Liberty ad infinitum), or the design workshop's own *Spirale* (Spiral), a kind of *perpetuum mobile* frozen in crystal – works which primarily accentuate the beauty of the material itself. Some people may prefer the delicate, exquisitely crafted pieces of a century ago – as the cutters and engravers themselves may miss the challenge such pieces posed to the craftsman's skill – but Baccarat's most recent creations, seen alongside the old in the company's two museums, are a vivid testimony to a living creative force, a force that has been constantly changing, developing and renewing itself now for more than two hundred years.

Facing page: casket shown at the Exposition Universelle of 1878. The design is reminiscent of the silver-gilt Treasure of the Order of the Holy Ghost (16th century). Gilded bronze and crystal cut and wheel-engraved in motifs also inspired by Renaissance art, with ciboriums surmounted by bowls of fruit and horns of plenty.

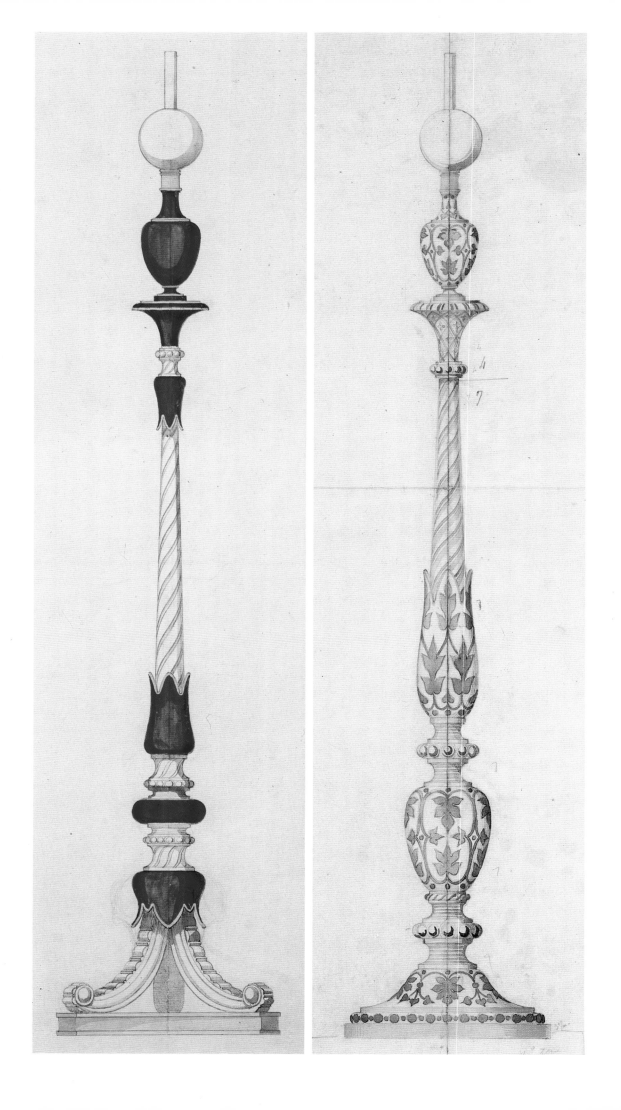

Page 84. TORCHÈRE POMPÉIENNE (Pompeiian Candelabrum), shown at the Exposition in Nancy (1909) and at the Musée Galliera, Paris (1910). Incorporating birds in combat with snakes, fauns' heads and lion-claw tripods, this model in crystal and chased and gilded bronze takes its inspiration from ancient Rome. The crystal basin, signed Pétremant, is engraved with a 'Triumph of Bacchus' consisting of fifteen figures, including several representations of Bacchus, Silenus and Bacchantes playing musical instruments. The design is a reproduction of a bas-relief made by the English sculptor John Flaxman for a series of vases and ornamental pieces in blue ceramic with white embossed figures manufactured by the Wedgwood company after 1777. The vase on page 201 is also engraved by Pétremant after a work by Flaxman and Wedgwood.

85. Detail of the candelabrum (page 84) showing one of the three electrified lamps, in cut crystal, in imitation of a Roman oil lamp, surmounted by a Cupid in gilded bronze playing with a goose.

86. Studies of gas lamp stands, c. 1860. Pencil drawings with gouache and watercolour on heavy paper.

87. Oil lamp or reliquary, shown at the Exposition Universelle of 1878. The Roman-inspired tripod, representing fauns' hooves, was made either in gilded bronze (as here) or with a satin finish. The lidded vase in pink cased crystal has been wheel-engraved with three scenes depicting either the child Bacchus or genies. Gilded bronze perfume cassolettes and silver-gilt table pieces by the goldsmith Odiot, in the same shape, also existed in the late 18th century.

88, 89. Large basin, one of a pair, shown at the Exposition Universelle of 1878. The crystal basin – in white opal crystal cased with cobalt-blue crystal – is encircled by a gilded bronze procession of twelve Cupids joined by a garland of flowers. The two large Cupids on either side carry torches consisting of six candlesticks embellished with cut-crystal drops. The bronze designs evoke the art of the Renaissance, particularly architectural stucco designs executed in Florence in the 16th century. A removable container in embossed and gilded brass fits inside the basin.

91. CAVE ELÉPHANT (Elephant Liqueur Cabinet), shown at the Exposition Universelle of 1878. This liqueur cabinet is inspired by the Elephant of the Bastille, a monumental fountain in bronze and stone commissioned by Napoleon from the architect Jean-Antoine Alavoine in 1808. The project was abandoned, but the wood and plaster model remained at the Bastille until 1846. A 'symbol of popular strength' according to Victor Hugo, the Elephant influenced a number of the 19th century's artistic creations. The Elephant Cabinet is made of moulded, etched, frosted, cut and gilded crystal and gilded bronze. Four liqueur decanters fit into the palanquin, and twelve small glasses with handles hang from the bronze harness. Only a few models were made in the 19th century, but the piece has recently been reissued.

Table and nef reissued in two copies in 1989 from 19th-century models. Two or perhaps three such rectangular tables were made in 1889. In 1927 an article in the magazine *Art et Industrie* mentions that there were two of these tables in Baroness d'Erlanger's Paris apartment. In 1978 the Corning Museum of Glass (USA) acquired a table and nef at the Drouot auction rooms, and the Los Angeles Museum of Art acquired another table in 1989.

Two copies of the nef were commissioned by the Grand Dépôt, a famous department store opened in Paris on Rue Drouot in 1863 and nicknamed 'the palace of the *arts du feu*'. The nef, which was designed by the sculptor Charles Vital-Cornu (1851–1927), was to symbolize the city of Paris at the Exposition Universelle of 1900.
At the prow a child kneels on a chimera and gazes towards the horizon, while another child in gilded bronze unfastens the boat's moorings so that it can be cast out into the dawning 20th century (see detail, opposite). One of the two nefs made in 1900 was kept at Baccarat as a kind of mascot until 1930, when it was sold to Sir Ganga Singhji Bahadur, Maharajah of Bikaner and a member of the League of Nations, for his Hindu palace of Lallgarh.

JETS D'EAU ('Fountains') chandelier, designed by Georges Chevalier,
and luminous columns, c. 1925.

Facing page: CANDÉLABRE DU TSAR (Tsar Candelabrum), c. 1905. This candelabrum
(height: 3.85 m/12 ft 5 in.), consisting of 79 electric bulbs, was probably created for the
Russian imperial court between 1905 and 1910 and shown at the Exposition in Nancy in 1909.

Page 97. Glass from a water set, 1831. The bowl is funnel-shaped and moulded with bamboos. A punty (or roundel) is cut into each shoot and a star is cut under the foot.

■

98, 99. 'Still Life with Butterfly': EMPIRE glasses and decanter; enamelled fruit dish (c. 1880); crystal and bronze candlestick (end 19th century); serving dish with stand in crystal and bronze (1904); enamelled and gilded hock glass (1909); plates and bowls in Limoges porcelain commissioned by Editions Paradis; cup and saucer in Sèvres porcelain; and a *Trogonoptera Brookiana*, a bird butterfly from Malaysia (F. Satger collection).

■

100. HARCOURT water glass, with heavy crystal funnel-shaped bowl, triple-knopped stem, hexagonal foot, and six large flat cuts just beneath the rim. This table service, designed in 1841, boasts an exceptional longevity: introduced in the 1910 catalogue, it has been reissued ever since. The presidencies of Brazil (1952), Lebanon (1955) and the Ivory Coast (1959) and the King of Cambodia (1961) ordered it, engraved and gilded with their arms and monograms, and the Shah of Iran used it for the banquet tables during the Festival of Persepolis in 1971, on the occasion of the 2,500th anniversary of the Persian Empire. The presidency of the French Republic uses the service for large dinners held outside the Elysée palace, such as in the Galerie des Glaces at Versailles, and the service is also used in France's largest embassies, notably in England and the United States.

■

101. Water glass, c. 1844. Funnel-shaped bowl cut with six long, wide flat cuts. On the stem, a knop is cut in facets in *bleu céleste* agate glass. A blazing star is cut under the foot.

■

102. Water glass, 1858. The funnel-shaped bowl is cut with flat cuts and threads, with a wheel-engraved garland of flowers beneath the rim. The blown and cut stem is baluster-shaped with a knop; the foot is cut with festoons and olives.

■

103. Water glass, c. 1863. The Empire-style palmettes and water leaves were first etched, then wheel-engraved. A frieze runs beneath the rim and the olives have been polished with a lead wheel. This glass is a fine example of the early uses of chemical engraving, which served to imprint a particularly elaborate design prior to wheel-engraving.

■

Study for a novelty glass, for the Exposition Universelle of 1878. Pencil drawing with ink wash and gouache on heavy paper, inspired by 16th-century Venetian glassware.

Facing page: tulip-shaped goblet with foot, for a water set, c. 1865. Silver cementation (producing an amber colour) has been used to paint threads and a medallion on clear crystal. After annealing, a Bohemian-style hunting scene was etched on the medallion.

Calyx-shaped glass, 1878. The shape is similar to that of 17th-century German glasswork. The stem has been blown and modelled with tongs and the foot is bordered. The design is wheel-engraved, with mat motifs heightened with shiny beads.

BEAUNE, champagne flute, c. 1880. Gilded embossed design.

Facing page: water glass, from a water set shown at the Exposition Universelle of 1867. The bowl and foot have been wheel-engraved with a Louis XV-style design of furled acanthus leaves, garlands of flowers and diamond motifs. The baluster-shaped stem has been blown and cut.

The cutting of heavy crystal, much in vogue during the decades leading up to 1860, was gradually abandoned in favour of etching and wheel-engraving, which became the principal decorative techniques for a great number of items. Crystal became increasingly thin (mousseline or muslin glass), and wheel-engraving at Baccarat, developed after 1839 with the arrival of engravers from Bohemia, reached its peak at the Expositions Universelles of 1867 and 1878.

VALLÉE, water glass, 1902. Alternating baskets of flowers and fruit, in the Louis XV style, have been cut and partially polished by wheel-engraving.

Water glass, 1887. Elongated funnel-shaped bowl with a Japanese-style intaglio design of apple and pine branches, creating a tapestry-like composition that gives a feeling of depth and luxuriance.

Facing page: wine glass, 1896. The unfurling plants and large wading bird taking flight evoke Renaissance decorative motifs. The technique used here – stone-wheel intaglio and acid polishing – accentuates the impression of high-relief and is reminiscent of intaglio engraving on precious stones or lithophane impressions on porcelain.

Page 108. Water glass, c. 1880. Balloon-shaped bowl in mousseline crystal; stem cut with two knops and foot cut in the shape of a star. Louis XV-style gilded embossed design.

■

109. LORIENT, water glass, 1889. Heavy cut-crystal bowl in broken diamond motif. The second half of the 19th century revived the fashion for heavily cut designs with rich and complex motifs. In the period 1874–1914 Baccarat employed a record number of workers (over 2,000) in order to meet the demand for rich cut-glass designs.

■

112. BEAUNE, water glass, c. 1880. Blown foot with a border, and tulip-shaped bowl. The Beaune service was shown at the Exposition Universelle of 1878. It was reissued up until the middle of the 20th century in a variety of gilded or wheel-engraved versions. Undecorated, it was often gilded with monograms or coats of arms. Here, it bears a gilded embossed design similar to the gilded bronze decorations on the large blue crystal basins shown at the Exposition Universelle of 1878.

■

114. Water glass, 1900. Bowl cut with bezels and rosettes, on a baluster-shaped stem with a knop. A star is cut under the foot.

■

115. Water glass, 1900. Conical-shaped bowl finely cut with bezels, diamonds and rosettes, with a wheel-engraved and polished twining brier running beneath the rim. Cut stem with a blown knop and a star cut under the foot.

■

116. Hock glass, 1904. A woman's portrait has been wheel-engraved on the bowl together with engraved and polished stylized plant motifs. The long stem is made of four cut segments, one of which consists of two spiralling threads of moss-coloured crystal. A circular frieze is engraved on the foot.

■

117. Hock glass, 1904. Detail of the wheel-engraved woman's portrait on the bowl.

■

Water glass, 1926. Flowers, foliage and threads are painted in gold on the bowl and foot.
The gold of the flowers has been left mat, while that of the foliage has been burnished
with an agate stone.

Hock glass, shown at the Exposition in Nancy in 1909. It has a cut stem with a knop and a star
cut under the foot. The bowl is painted in gilded embossed enamels in the style of Islamic
glasswork of the 13th and 14th centuries and pottery designs from Iznik and Damascus.

Facing page: CALICE wine glass. The service was shown at the Exposition in Nancy in 1909. The
tall blown stem gives this glass the delicate look of 17th-century Venetian glassware. The design
has been wheel-engraved and partially polished.

MASSÉNA, water glass, 1979. The bowl is cut with bezels. The Masséna service was
Baccarat's greatest commercial success in the United States during the 1980s.

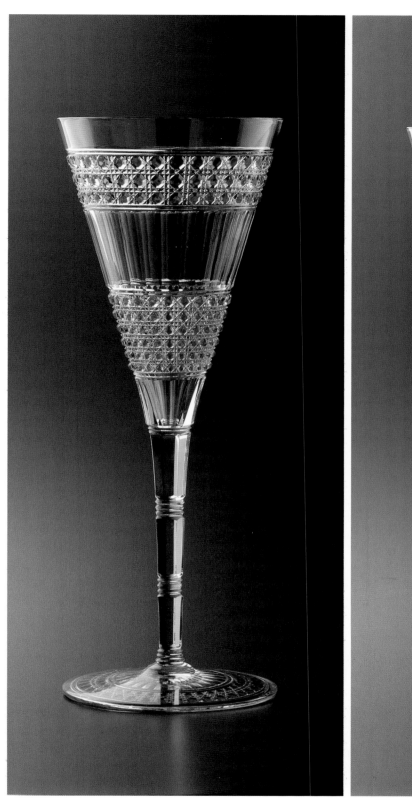

FLERS, water glass. Service shown at the Exposition in Nancy in 1909. Clear crystal cased with pink crystal. The glass is cut with alternating flat cuts, threads and diamond stone designs. Only the diamond stones have retained the thin layer of coloured crystal.

FLERS, water glass, 1909. Clear crystal version of the above. Cased crystal glasses were more expensive than the clear versions.

Hock glass, 1928. Bowl cased with green crystal and cut with fir-tree designs.

KERNEVEL, hock glass, 1911. Bowl in deep orange crystal cut with large diamond-shaped bezels; cut stem and foot.

Facing page: SERVICE DU TSAR (Tsar Service), water glass, 1909. In cased crystal, entirely cut, the service was made, in a choice of colours, for the Russian market. Each of the six glasses of the service has its own individual shape.

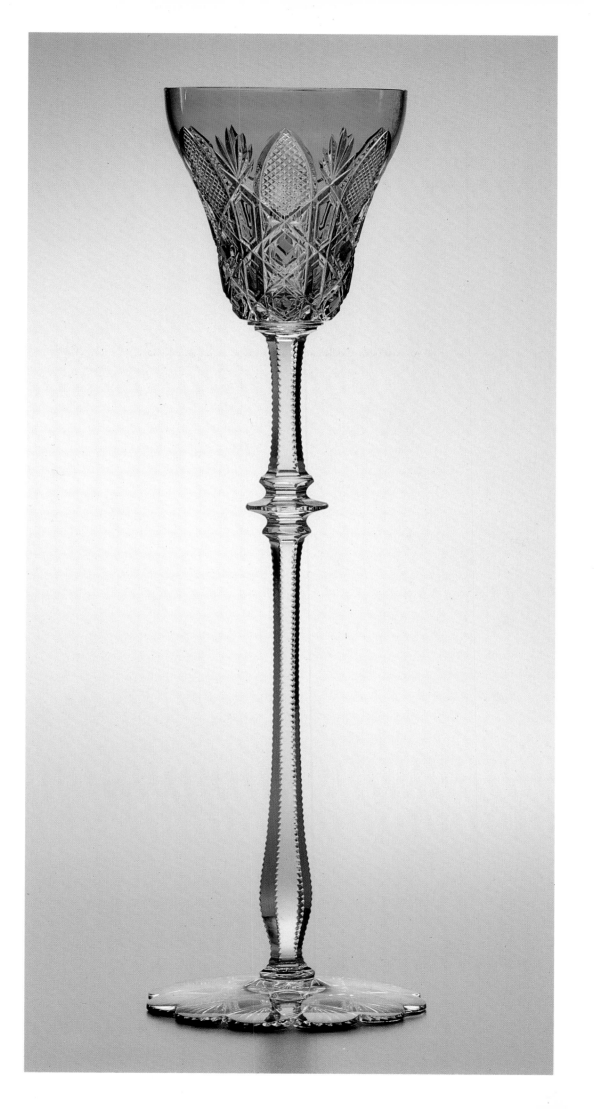

Page 124. BRUNO PAUL, wine glass, 1913. Tulip-shaped bowl with elongated flat cuts; cut stem with knop and a star under the foot.

126. Champagne glass, 1910–20. Cut stem; bowl etched with a garland of flowers and ribbons in Louis XVI style. The etched motifs have been gilded and painted with embossed turquoise-blue and orange enamels.

127. VOLNAY, water glass, 1924. The bowl is etched, gilded and enamelled in the decorative style of the 1920s.

130. 'An American Woman in Paris': glasses in mousseline crystal (1937); fruit dish (1925); statuette of Josephine Baker by Georges Chevalier (1929) with a plaster study (1928–29); black crystal vase (1924); BANANA paperweight; ORSAY candlestick; presentation plate and ISADORA DUNCAN plate by Raynaud; ATLANTIDE silverware by Christofle.

MALADETTA, water glass. Service designed by Georges Chevalier in 1947. The heavy square-sectioned stem represents the highest massif of the Pyrenees.

FRUCTIDOR, Madeira glass. Service designed by Georges Chevalier and shown at the Exposition Internationale des Arts Décoratifs in 1925. Plain bowl and foot in the shape of a truncated pyramid, with citrus fruits sculpted in bas-relief by a process of moulding and frosting the foot's inner surface.

Facing page: LES JETS D'EAU (The Water Fountain), liqueur glass. Table service designed by Georges Chevalier for the Baccarat-Christofle pavilion at the Exposition Internationale des Arts Décoratifs in 1925. The bowl is etched with fountain motifs; the stem is decorated with blown and frosted flowers, and a wave-like design has been blown on the foot.
The model was reissued in 1991.

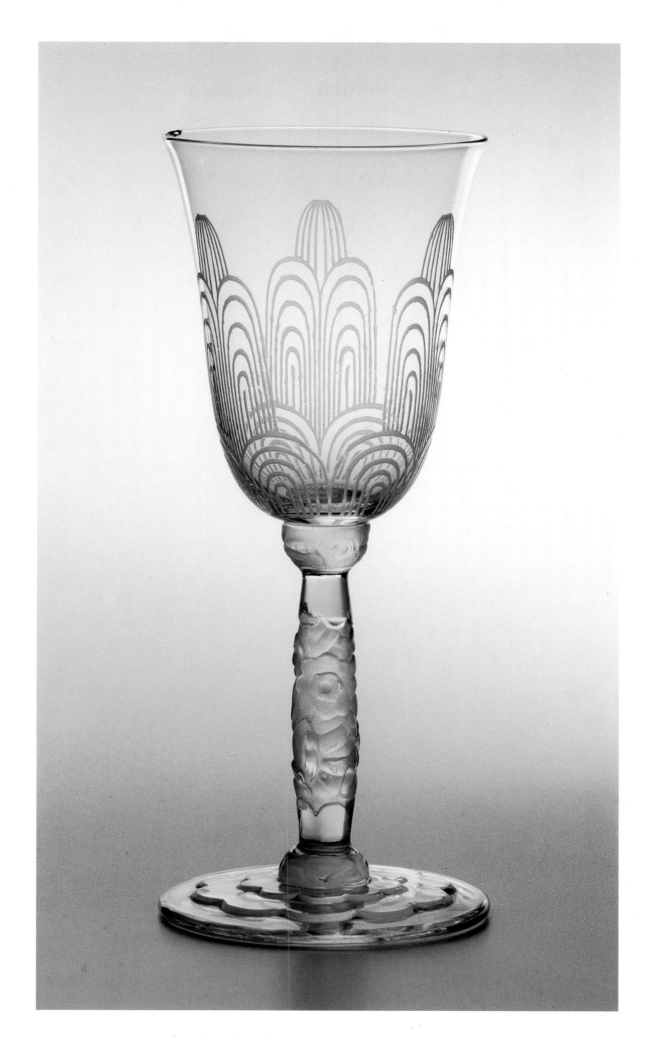

JEAN BART, water glass. Service called POUR LE YACHT (For the Yacht) with engraved design by Georges Chevalier, 1930; shown (without the design) at the Exposition Internationale des Arts Décoratifs in 1925. The three-masted ships and anchors are wheel-engraved on the plain crystal bowl. The square foot and absence of a stem lower the glass's centre of gravity and ensure its excellent stability, even in stormy weather.

Water glass, shown at the Exposition Universelle of 1937. The stem and circular foot were first blown and cut, then joined to the tulip-shaped bowl while the crystal was still hot.

SAINT-ETIENNE, claret glass, 1934.
The bowl has been cut with a band
of mat diamond shapes between
blown ribbons.

PLOMBIÈRE, plain crystal glass,
for port or cocktails, 1936.

CHAMPS-ELYSÉES, claret glass, 1934.
Etched bowl on a short cut stem.

ORSAY, water glass. Service designed by Thomas Bastide
in 1988. The delicate round bowl has a solid, heavily cut
hexagonal base.

BAIN D'OEIL (Eye Bath), claret glass designed by Georges
Chevalier and exhibited at the Exposition Universelle
of 1937. Inspired by a crystal eye bath made by Baccarat
in 1878.

Water glass designed by Georges Chevalier and shown
at the Exposition Universelle of 1937. The spherical
bowl has been heat-joined to the rectangular stem and
foot in moulded and cut crystal.

Page 132. ATLANTIC, hock glass, 1930. Named after the deluxe hotel opened in Nice in 1914; in moss-coloured crystal cut in large facets.

133. MAJESTIC, claret glass, 1929. Named after the deluxe hotel opened in Cannes in 1926; with a plain bowl on a cut stem and foot.

135. SAINT-HUBERT, claret glass, 1935. Bowl with flat cuts, heat-joined to the black crystal stem, which has been moulded and recut. A version exists in clear crystal.

137. Cocktail glass, shown at the Exposition Universelle of 1937. Moulded double stem and rectangular foot, cut and heat-joined to the bowl, which is cut with four large flat cuts.

139. 'Boulevard du Rhum': glasses by Georges Chevalier (1937); spherical decanter (1930); POUR LE YACHT (For the Yacht) jug by Georges Chevalier (1925); candle-holder for three candles (1937); flower vase (1936); ANNEAU D'OR (Gold Ring) plate by Raynaud and ATLANTIDE silverware by Christofle.

141. AURELLE DE PALADINES, water glass. Service shown at the Exposition Universelle of 1937. Bowl in mousseline crystal; stem with blown, cut knop.

142. Water glass, shown at the Exposition Universelle of 1937. Plain bowl in mousseline crystal; stem with four knops formed with tongs.

143. LECZINSKA, water glass. Shown at the Exposition Universelle of 1937. Mousseline crystal bowl with a blown stem shaped with tongs.

144. AVILA, water glass. Shown at the Exposition Universelle of 1937. Conical bowl in mousseline crystal on a straight stem cut with three hexagonal knops.

145. Water glass, designed by Georges Chevalier in 1939. Tulip-shaped bowl in mousseline crystal. Square stem with four narrow flat cuts and a flat knop in the shape of an eight-pointed star. The rim of the foot has been cut with bezels.

JOSÉ, water glass. Service designed by Boris Tabacoff in 1970. The cylindrical bowl contrasts with the solid stem in the shape of a teardrop.

BOUQUET, hock glass, 1971. One of six plain crystal glasses designed by Robert Rigot in different colours and heights. Each glass is made from a single piece of crystal, the stem being drawn from the bowl while the mixture is still hot.

Facing page: NEPTUNE, water glass. Service designed by Thomas Bastide in 1987. Three long flat cuts are drawn from the stem to the bowl and the upper part of the bowl is made up of six narrow bezels that reach all the way to the rim.

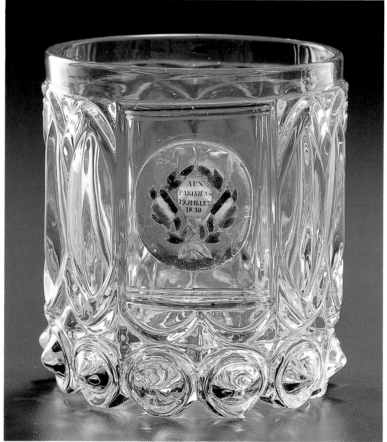

Moulded tumbler 'with points', c. 1830. The bouquet
of flowers, enamelled on gold foil, is cased
in the cut-crystal inset.

Moulded goblet 'with escutcheons and points', c. 1831.
The commemorative flag of the three revolutionary days
of 1830, enamelled on gold foil, is cased
in the cut-crystal inset.

Beaune, water glass. Blown bowl, stem and foot in mousseline crystal with the French coat of arms wheel-engraved and gilded on the bowl. The piece was commissioned for the Duke of Aosta in 1897.

Beaune, water glass, undated. Coat of arms painted with multicoloured enamels.

SERVICE DE L'ELYSÉE (Elysée Service), water glass. This service, decorated with a 'cut-glass floating diamond shape' design, was exhibited at the Exposition Universelle of 1867. President Félix Faure, former Minister of the Navy and of the French Colonies, had its oval medallion engraved with his initials cased with an anchor. His successor, Emile Loubet, ordered the service in 1899, engraved with the initials of the French Republic (as here). The service is still used at state banquets at the Elysée palace.

Marshal Joffre's service at Army General Headquarters, water glass, 1915. The victory wreath painted with a mixture of translucent and opaque enamels consists of intertwined laurel and holly wound round with a tricolour ribbon and symbolizes Marshal Joffre's national renown after his victory on the Marne.

Water glass, 1934. Funnel-shaped bowl on a short, slender stem. The medallion is wheel-engraved with the coat of arms of the Countess of Paris.

Facing page: 'Prix Goncourt': JUVISY decanter and glasses; NAPOLÉON cognac glass; RÉGENCE candelabrum; wheel-engraved flower vase (1878); LOUVECIENNES dinner plate by Haviland; ALLIANCE presentation plate by Bernardaud; MARLY silverware by Christofle.

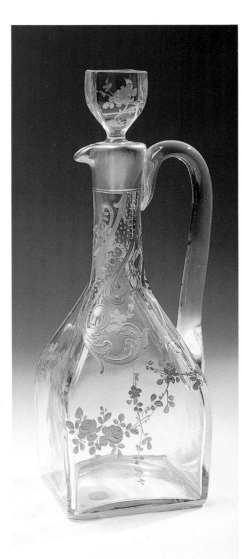

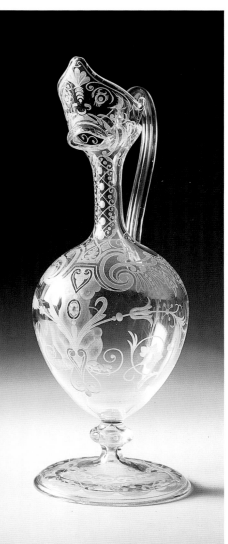

AIGUIÈRE DE LOUIS DE BOURBON (Louis de Bourbon Ewer), 1828. On 12 September 1828 King Charles X, his eldest son, the dauphin Louis de Bourbon, and his Prime Minister, Jean-Baptiste Martignac, visited the Baccarat crystalworks during a tour of eastern France. The royal visitors received a number of gifts, including this crystal ewer, which was presented to the dauphin by the manager. An enamelled gold jewel representing the coats of arms of France and Navarre is cased in the inset. Created by a jeweller in Louis XVI style, the jewel incorporates the three fleurs-de-lys (curiously reversed in relation to their usual position), the chains of Navarre, the necklaces of the Orders of Saint-Michael and of the Holy Spirit, and the double L and royal crown. The body of the ewer has been blown and the lip flame-opened. The stem and foot were applied and fashioned while the crystal was still hot. The perfect positioning of the jewel within the crystal makes this piece a rare feat of glassmaking. The foot is plain, in contrast to the richly decorated body, which may mean that the ewer was incomplete and merely a trial piece for the one that was actually given to the dauphin.

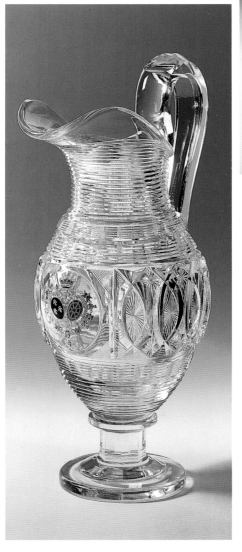

Liqueur decanter, 1895. The trapezium shape and square base are reproduced on the stopper. Louis XV-style gilded embossed design.

Ewer, exhibited at the Exposition Universelle of 1867. In crystal mousseline, with lip cut with shears and formed when hot. The handle and foot, which is decorated with a border, have been blown separately, then attached to the body. The Renaissance-style chimera and arabesques are wheel-engraved.

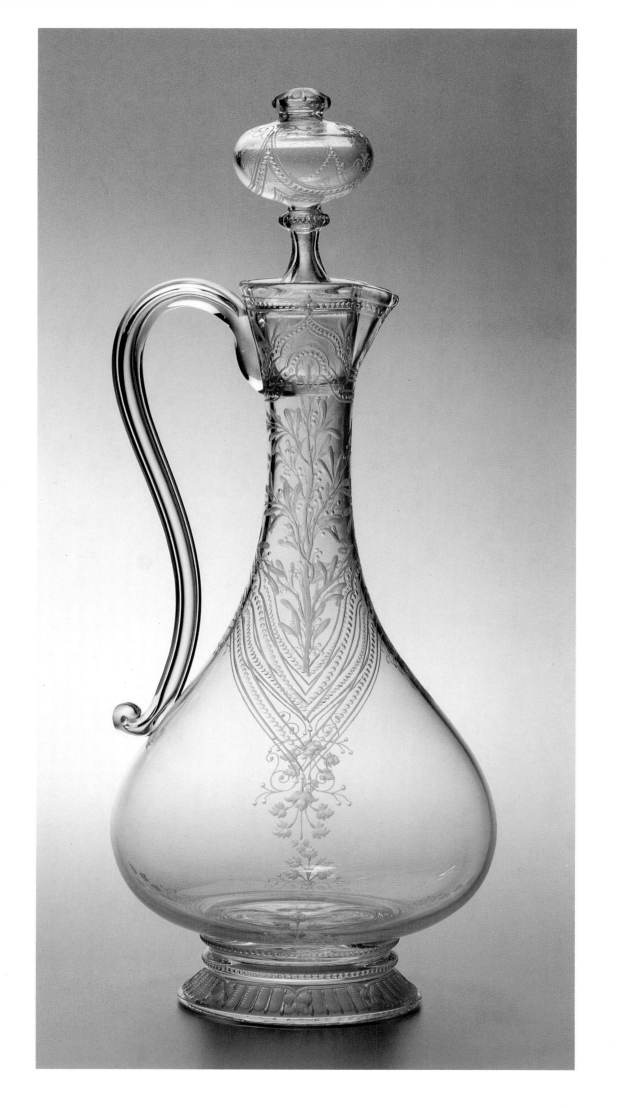

Decanter, shown at the
Exposition in Nancy in 1909.
The decorative motifs are carved
in intaglio and polished by
etching.

Decanter, shown at the Exposition in
Nancy in 1909. Wheel-engraved and
polished decorative motifs.

Facing page: stoppered wine jug, part
of a service, shown at the Exposition
Universelle of 1878. The stopper,
handle and foot have all been blown.
The Persian-style decorative motifs
are wheel-engraved.

Decanter, part of a service, shown at
the Exposition Universelle of 1878.
The foot has been blown separately,
then attached. The stopper has a
hollow plug and has been entirely
blown and fashioned with tongs. The
Renaissance-style decorative motifs
are wheel-engraved
(see detail, page 168).

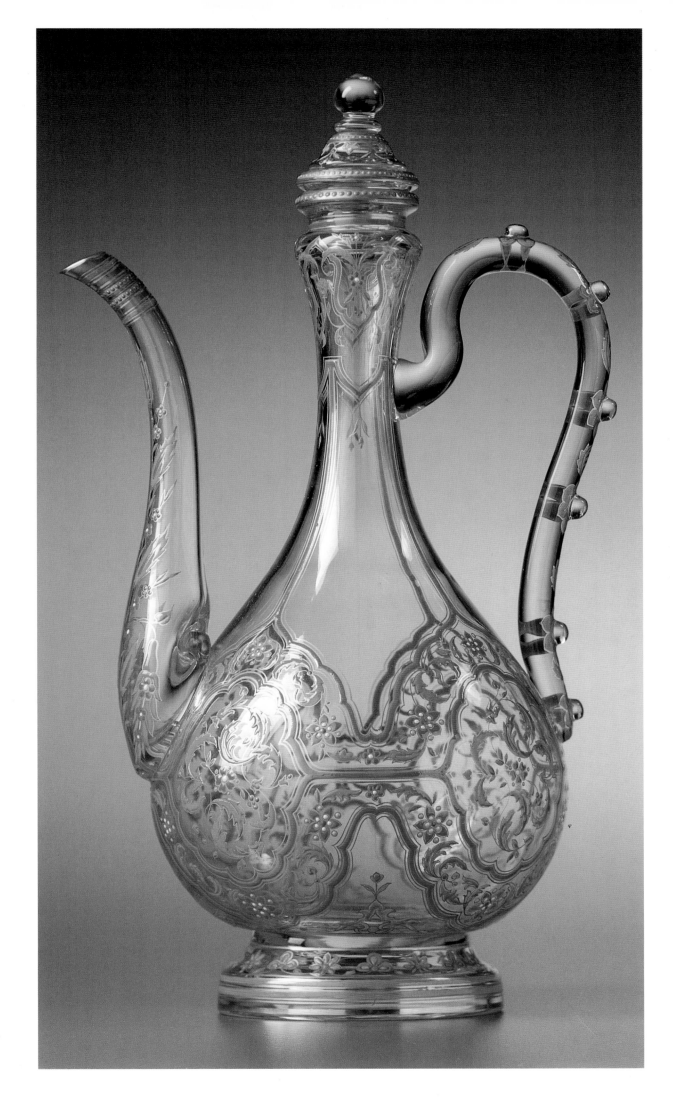

Page 172. Water jug, exhibited at the Exposition Universelle of 1878. Handle, lip and neck cut with facets; body cut with diamond-shaped bezels in escutcheons.

173. Coffee pot for a mocha service, shown at the Exposition Universelle of 1878. The lip, foot and lid have all been blown. The decorative motifs, executed in the manner of Persian miniatures, are reminiscent of Iznik porcelain motifs. The opaque enamels in turquoise, orange and white are outlined with a double gold thread, and the design, clearly Oriental in inspiration, revives the tradition of Islamic glasswork produced in Damascus in the 14th century. The service consists of eighteen pieces presented on a tray: coffee pot, sugar bowl, eight small cups, and eight 'zarfs', little glasses in the shape of egg cups used to hold the cups when they are filled with hot coffee.

174. Wine bottle for Johannisberg wines (Germany), 1887. Green crystal, with applied neck ring. The bottle is decorated with flat cuts and twisted olives.

175 (left). Stoppered wine jug shown at the Exposition in Nancy in 1909. The Empire-style design is carved in intaglio and has been polished by means of an acid bath.

175 (right). Jug for beer or orangeade, shown at the Exposition in Nancy in 1909. The design is carved in intaglio and has been polished by means of an acid bath.

'Marabout' or round-lipped water jug, c. 1833. In moulded crystal with a 'diamonds and leaves' design and bezels cut on the neck and handle; the lip formed with shears. Used for washing the hands before and after meals, the 'marabout' came with a matching basin.

Dessert dish, c. 1835. Moulded in two heat-joined parts. Hollow foot and flared dish with a 'sand-blasted diamond and arabesque' design.

Decanter, undated. Richly cut in the style of Baccarat designs from the beginning of the 20th century.

Decanter, part of a service, c. 1835. Cylindrical body with an applied ring. The stopper has been blown and cut. On the lower part of the body, the 'sand-blasted arabesque' design has been moulded, while the upper part is decorated with flat cuts and threads.

Facing page: stoppered jug, part of a service, 1858. The neck has an applied ring and the body is decorated with olives and flat cuts and wheel-engraved vine leaves and grapes.

Page 165. Six-piece water set (the small orange-water decanter is missing), exhibited at the Exposition Universelle of 1867. The bowls, stoppers, feet and knops are in blown mousseline crystal. The decorative motifs, consisting of scrolls and leaves taken from 17th-century designs, are wheel-engraved and partially polished. The neck of the decanter and the glass stems are cut with facets and beads, giving a luminous effect.

166. Decanter, part of a service, shown at the Exposition Universelle of 1878. Mousseline crystal. The blown stopper has a hollow plug, and the foot has been blown, then applied to the stem. The Renaissance-style decorative motifs are wheel-engraved.

167 (left). Stoppered wine jug, part of a service, exhibited at the Exposition Universelle of 1878. The handle and foot have been blown separately, then attached. The stopper has a hollow plug and has been entirely blown and fashioned with tongs. The decorative motifs are wheel-engraved and partially polished, inspired, like the shape of the jug, by Renaissance ewers in pewter and gold.

167 (right). Stoppered wine jug, part of a service, exhibited at the Exposition Universelle of 1878. The handle and foot have been blown separately, then attached. The stopper has a hollow plug and has been entirely blown and fashioned with tongs. The Renaissance motifs are wheel-engraved and partially polished (see detail, page 169).

168. Decanter, part of a service, shown at the Exposition Universelle of 1878 (detail of page 171). The foot has been blown separately, then attached. The wheel-engraved sea monsters and chimeras surrounded by leafy scrolls are taken from Renaissance decorative motifs.

169. Detail of page 167: mousseline crystal with wheel-engraved motifs, 1878.

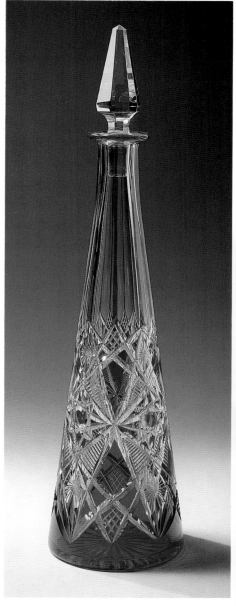

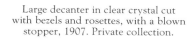
Large decanter in clear crystal cut with bezels and rosettes, with a blown stopper, 1907. Private collection.

Novelty decanter for fine wines, 1905. Clear crystal cased with pink crystal, cut with bezels, rosettes, flat cuts and stars.

Stoppered wine jug, 1906. Clear crystal cased with moss-coloured crystal, cut with decorative motifs. Private collection.

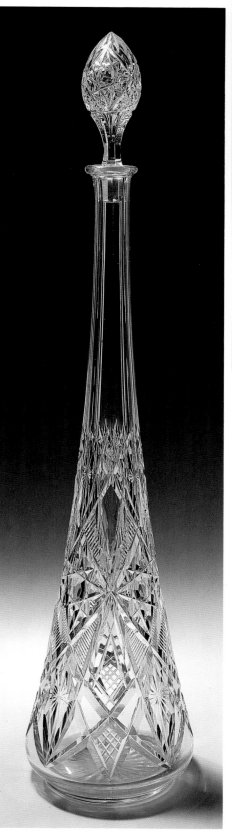

CHAMONIX, decanter, part of a service, 1930. Constructed in staggered hexagonal shapes.

DAVOS, decanter, part of a service, 1930. Plain, spherical body with rectangular blown stopper, stem and foot.

Page 180. Coloured crystal beads used to decorate millefiori paperweights.

181. Paperweights, from left to right and from top to bottom: 'Macédoine' (Medley; mid-19th century); 'Bouquet de Mariée' (Bridal Bouquet; mid-19th century); millefiori (1848); sulphide against a cobalt-blue background, with a portrait of Queen Elizabeth II of England sculpted by Gilbert Poillerat in 1954, unique specimen; sulphide with a portrait of John F. Kennedy sculpted by Albert David in 1963; camomile flower and beads (mid-19th century); 'Macédoine' (Medley; mid-19th century); butterfly and beads (mid-19th century); scattering of beads against a filigree background (mid-19th century).

182. Making paperweights.

183. Paperweights (1847–60) from the Corning Museum of Glass, New York, from left to right and from top to bottom: red primrose; blue, white and red primrose (1848); pansy and beads; 'Bouquet de Mariée' (Bridal Bouquet); flat bouquet with red rose and bud, pansy and double white clematis; red and white dahlia (all repeated below). In the centre, Cupid encircled by a wreath of beads on a red and opal background (c. 1849).

184. Paperweights, from left to right and from top to bottom: green snake (1979); green dragonfly and yellow flower (1982); pink butterfly (1978); sulphide on a hexagonal base, with portraits of the Marquis de La Fayette and George Washington, made in 1988 to commemorate the bicentenary of the French Revolution (copies of this paperweight were given to President Ronald Reagan and Vice-President George Bush by René de Chambrun, chairman of Baccarat); ruby waterlily and green frog (1981); salamander (1972–73); squirrel and beads (1971–73); 'Scorpio' and 'Sagittarius', on cobalt-blue backgrounds, sculpted by Gilbert Poillerat in 1955 (reissues).

185. Coloured crystal rods to be used to make beads for millefiori paperweights.

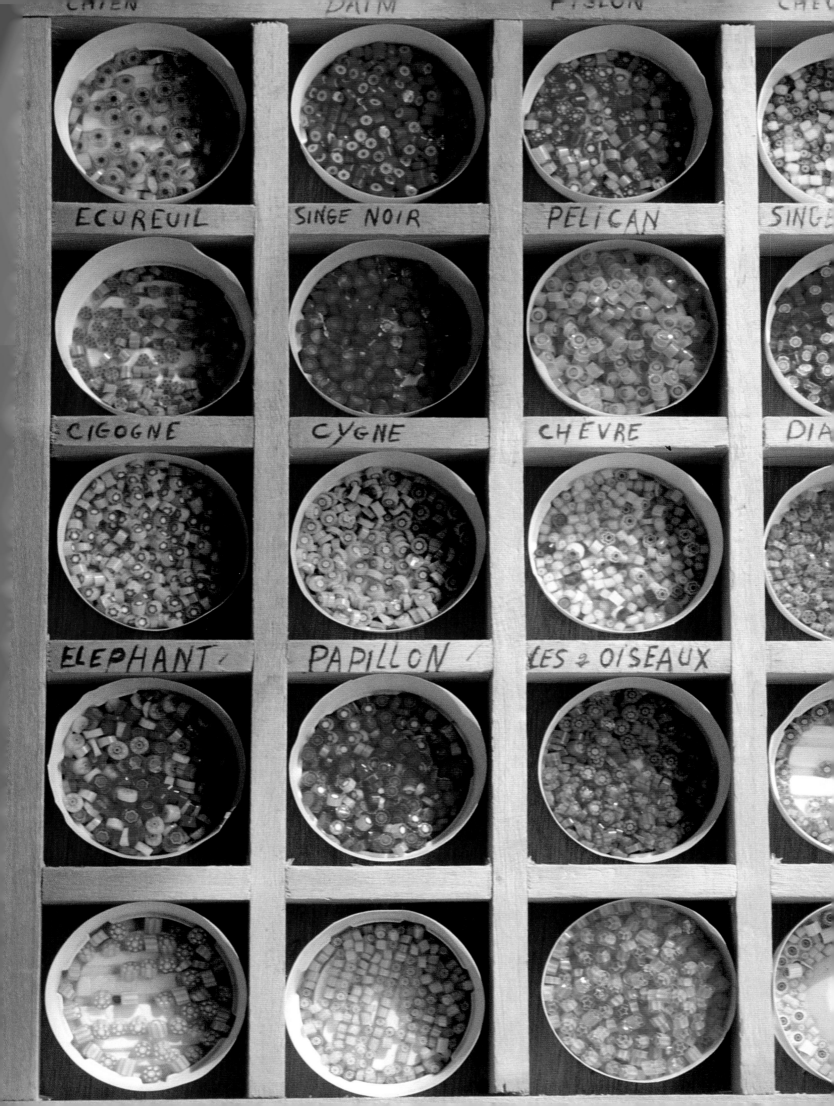

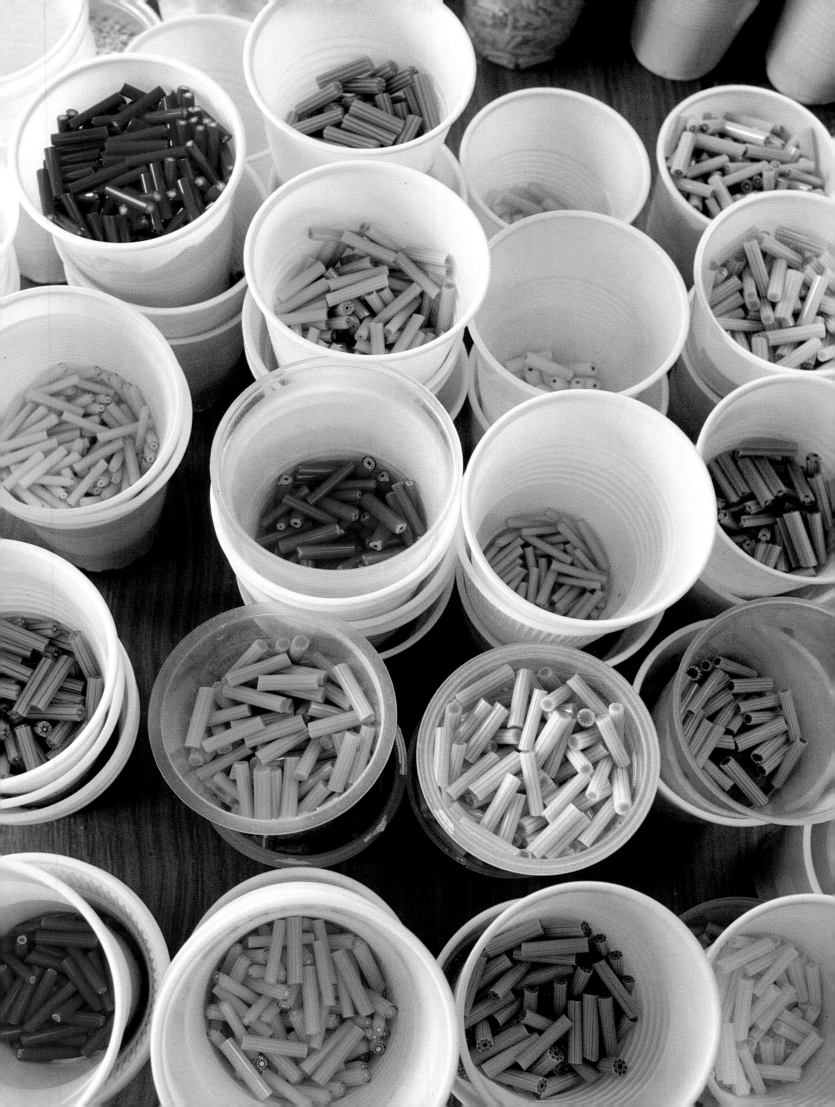

Liqueur service, c. 1882. In clear and turquoise-blue crystal. Eight four-lobed glasses with handles
and a spherical decanter on a rectangular tray. The design is painted with opaque enamels and
gilded. Private collection.

Water set, c. 1897. Six-piece set in clear and orangey-pink crystal (the colour obtained with gold salts) with Venetian cuts. Rococo motifs in gilded embossed design. Private collection.

Toiletry set, c. 1885. Clear crystal cased with moss-coloured crystal, decorated with hollow cuts and star-shaped diamonds; star base. From left to right: cylindrical powder box with knopped lid, cylindrical bottles with blown stoppers (two sizes) and oval-shaped tooth-powder box.

Compote dish, 'Jacques'-style glasses, and orangeade jug, 1881. This service, in crystal with a light amber-coloured lustre glaze, is painted with heavy multicoloured enamels and gilded. It is an example of the fashion for Japanese-inspired motifs taken from albums of Japanese engravings and illustrated books following the exhibitions of Japanese art at the Expositions Universelles of 1867 and 1878. Glassmaker-artists Eugène Rousseau (1827–90), Emile Gallé (1846–1904) and Félix Bracquemond (1833–1914), like the designers at Baccarat, were fond of these Japanese-style works.

Decanter, part of a water set, c. 1881. The crystal is covered with amber- or blue-tinted lustre glazes. The stopper has been shaped with tongs and the handle and four feet were made separately and attached. The 'heraldic' lion and plant motifs have been applied with opaque multicoloured enamels and gold and silver paint. The heraldic style, one of those adopted by Baccarat at the end of the 19th century, revives motifs from medieval and Renaissance art.

Sugar bowl, part of a water set,
1881–84. The Japanese-style design is
painted in multicoloured enamels
and in gold.

Sugar bowl, part of a water set,
1880–84. Decorated with a butterfly
embossed in multicoloured
enamels and gilded.

Alcohol lamp, c. 1890.
In pinkish-orange crystal
moulded with twisted
bamboos and decorated with
a chased silver-plated pewter
setting.

Travel bottle, c. 1885.
Cylindrical shape, with cut
neck and stopper and a star
cut into the base. The bottle
slips into a fitted ivory case
monogrammed with the
letter M in inlaid silver.
Private collection.

Egg-shaped box, 1895. White opal crystal, with threads and fleurs-de-lys painted in gold.

Study for a vase, January 1863. Pencil drawing on heavy paper with watercolours and gouache.

Facing page: water set, c. 1865. White opal crystal with enamelled neo-Grecian design,
partially frosted and gilded.

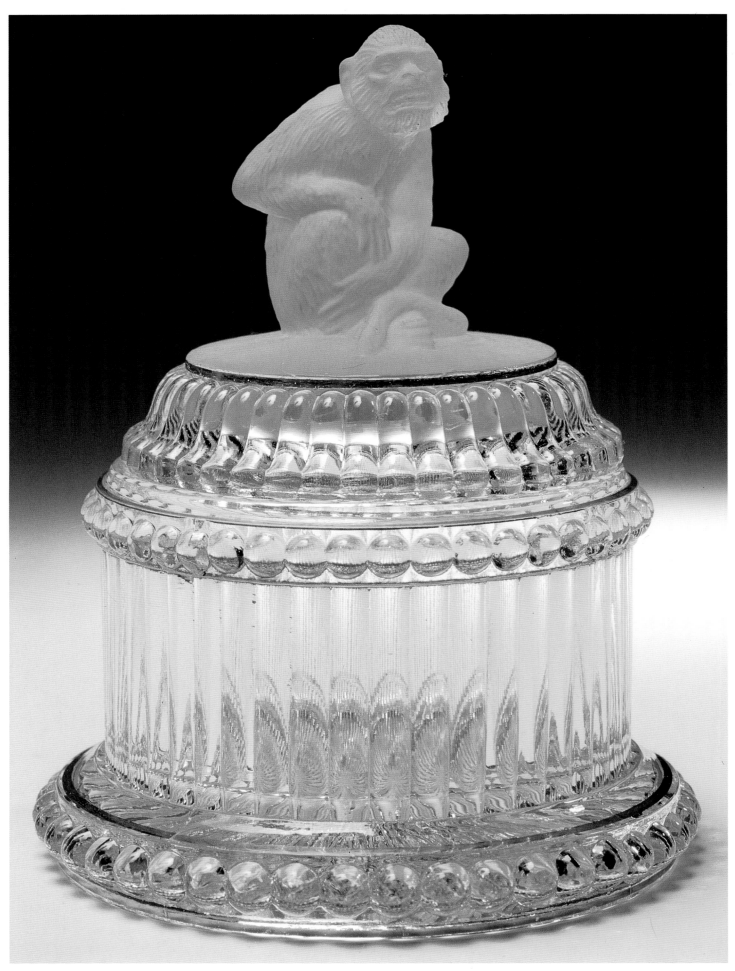

Sweet jar, 1872. Press-moulded crystal decorated with four gold threads. The knop of the lid,
representing a monkey, is frosted. The piece is part of a series of objects (including boxes, mirrors
and statuettes) produced after the Franco-Prussian War (1870–71) using frosted crystal,
a procedure which helped to mask any imperfections in the crystal.

Ice bucket, 1876. Press-moulded, frosted crystal, with a bas-relief reproducing a sacrificial scene from ancient Rome. The three lion-claw feet are also taken from neo-classical models.

Guy de Maupassant, ink well, 1989. Inspired by a model created in 1891, this hemispherical-shaped ink bottle is cut with curved bamboo motifs enclosing star-shaped diamonds. The base is cut with a 24-pointed star. Inside is a plain crystal container.

Ink well, 1891. Made in a press-mould, the inner cavity formed by
a nub inside the mould, then tightened with tongs. The outer surface
is cut with a garlanded bamboo motif on a background of star-shaped
diamonds. The chased and silvered metal lid is decorated with
bamboos. Private collection.

Ink well, c. 1903. Moulded crystal with large recut bamboos and
a 'marabout' (pot-bellied) lid in plain varnished bronze.

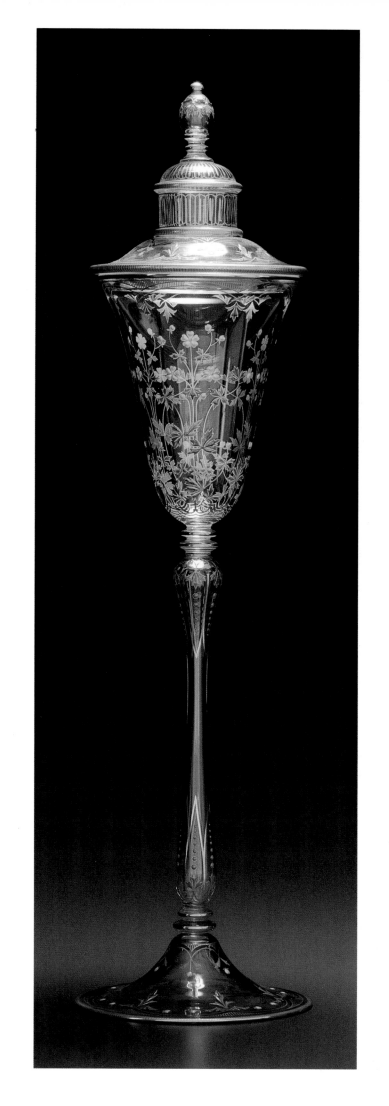

Page 198. Two-handled bottle decorated with wild geese, exhibited at the Exposition Universelle of 1878. Reproduction of a 'feeding-bottle' in rock crystal (now in the Louvre), a purely decorative piece dating from the reign of François I (16th century), part of the Royal Treasury. The shape of this bottle, which has a small metal spout at the base of the bulge, derives from Chinese teapots.

199. Chalice with lid, exhibited at the Exposition Universelle of 1878. Reproduction in wheel-engraved crystal of a rock-crystal vase of German origin from the 16th century.

200. Lobed fan-shaped bowl, with foot, shown at the Exposition Universelle of 1878. Reproduction of an engraved rock-crystal bowl, part of a collection of 16th-century pieces in precious materials now in the Louvre.

201. Vase, exhibited at the Exposition in Nancy (1909) and the Musée Galliera, Paris (1910). It is shaped like the 'ambrosia bowls' made in Silesia around 1730–60. (Ambrosia, the mythical food of the Olympian gods, was said to be nine times sweeter than honey, and to bestow immortality on those who ate it.) The oval shape, scalloped rim, fishtail handle and rococo-style decoration are typical of these bowls. This model in crystal was shown at the Exposition Universelle of 1878, then reissued in 1909 with a wheel-engraving attributed to Pétremant depicting ten nymphs dancing a Round of Hours, in the style of frescoes discovered at Herculaneum in the mid-18th century. The figures derive from decorative motifs found on the blue pottery with white embossed designs made by the Wedgwood company in 1776 after a bas-relief by the sculptor John Flaxman.

206 (left). Chalice with lid, shown at the Exposition in Nancy in 1909. In mousseline crystal with blown lid, bowl and foot. The stem is in three drawn parts joined by a triple knop just above the foot. Executed in the 'Venetian manner', the chalice is decorated with a gilded embossed design.

206 (right). Chalice with lid, shown at the Exposition in Nancy in 1909. In mousseline crystal, with blown stem fashioned with tongs. Executed in the 'Venetian manner'. The design is painted with embossed multicoloured enamels and gold.

207. Chalice with lid, shown at the Exposition in Nancy in 1909. In mousseline crystal, with blown lid, bowl, stem and foot. The floral design was painted with embossed multicoloured enamels and gold. The neo-Gothic shape and enamelwork are reminiscent of Renaissance art and of Venetian glasswork from the 15th and 16th centuries.

209. 'Flacons de Cheminée' (Ornamental Bottles), a plate from one of Baccarat's sales catalogues, 1860. After 1862 Baccarat's factory mark was printed on each page of their sales catalogues.

Flacons de Cheminée

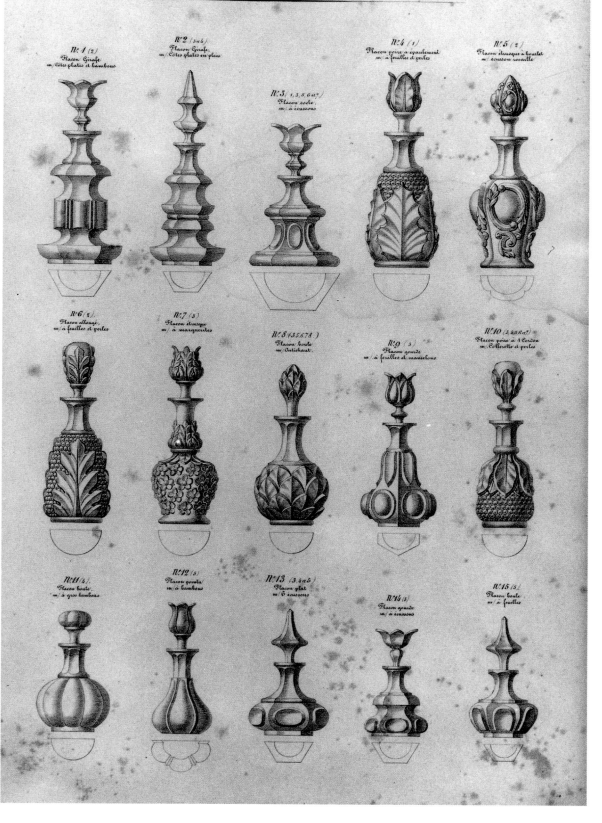

N: 1 (2)
Flacon Girafe
m/ Côtes plates et bambous

N: 2 (3n4)
Flacon Girafe,
m/ Côtes plates en plein

N: 3 (1, 3, 5, 6 n7)
Flacon socle,
m/ à écussons

N: 4 (1)
Flacon poire à épaulement
m/ à feuilles et perles

N: 5 (2)
Flacon étrusque à bourlet
m/ écusson rocaille

N: 6 (2)
Flacon allongé,
m/ à feuilles et perles

N: 7 (3)
Flacon étrusque
m/ à marguerites

N: 8 (4.3.5.6.7.8)
Flacon boule
m/ Artichaut

N: 9 (3)
Flacon gourde
m/ à feuilles et mamelons

N: 10 (3.4.5 n7)
Flacon poire à 4 cordon
m/ Collerette et perles

N: 11 (4)
Flacon boule
m/ à gros bambous

N: 12 (3)
Flacon gourde
m/ à bambous

N: 13 (3.4 n5)
Flacon plat
m/ 6 écussons

N: 14 (3)
Flacon gourde
m/ à écussons

N: 15 (3)
Flacon boule
m/ à feuilles

Ornamental bottle, c. 1844. Dichroic crystal (crystal whose colour – here green and yellow – depends on the angle of the light) coloured with uranium oxide. Experiments with colours obtained with uranium oxide were conducted at Baccarat by François-Eugène de Fontenay (1810–84), a graduate of the Ecole Centrale des Arts et Manufactures and winner of a prize awarded by the Société d'Encouragement pour l'Industrie Française in 1838 (for the colouring of glass). Glass coloured with uranium oxide has an even greater dichroism because of its low lead content.

Ornamental bottle, c. 1844. Clear crystal body with coloured crystal cabochons, applied and then facetted in imitation of precious stones.

Facing page: ornamental bottle, c. 1844. Clear crystal bottle and stopper decorated with *bleu céleste* agate glass cut in the shape of oval cabochons. The body of the bottle has also been cut.

Spherical bottle, moulded with 'leaf' designs, 1831.

MALMAISON, toiletry bottle, 1913. The stopper has been blown and the bottle itself decorated with flat cuts.

Ornamental bottle, c. 1855. Hoarfrost effect on crystal, achieved by applying crushed crystal to the clear crystal bowl while still hot. The bottle has been partially cut and painted with gold threads.

JASMIN (Jasmine), Mury, 1917.
Conical bottle with cobalt-blue
opaque enamel covering the neck and
spiralling down the body. Spherical
stopper with an emery finish.

CHYPRE MOUSSE (Cyprus Moss),
L. Legrand, 1917. Cylindrical bottle
with flattened round stopper and
emery finish, the design etched and
painted with opaque enamels in
orange and cobalt blue.

MITSOUKO, Guerlain, 1912, reissued
in 1947. The bottle, with its
'gendarme's cap' stopper, was
designed for the perfumes 'L'heure
bleue' and 'Fol arôme', then used in
1919 for 'Mitsouko'. Jacques
Guerlain took his inspiration from
Claude Farrère's novel *La Bataille*, in
which a British officer sent to fight in
the Russo-Japanese naval battle of
1905 finds himself powerfully
attracted to a Japanese woman by the
name of Mitsouko.

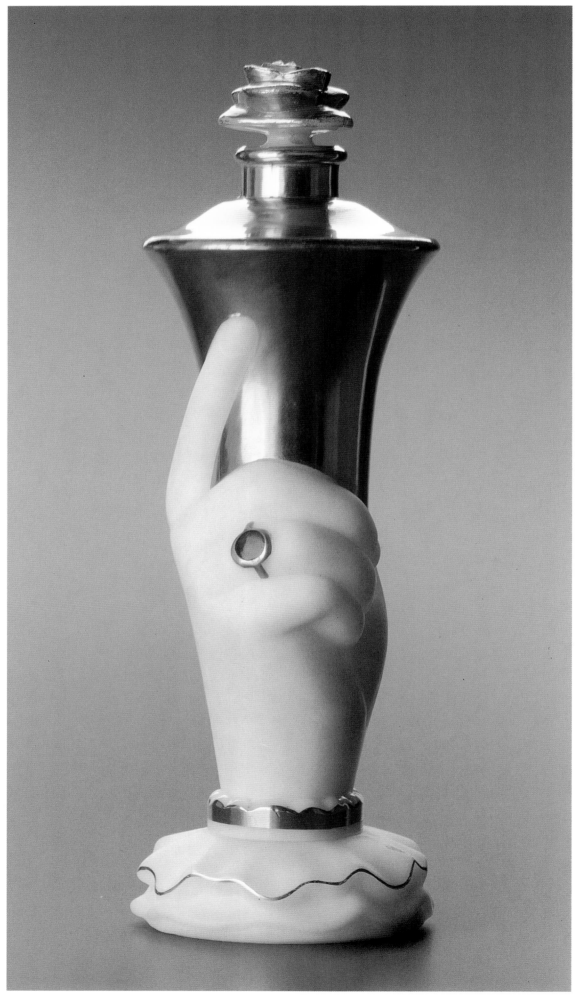

IT'S YOU, Elizabeth Arden, 1939. Bottle in white opal crystal representing a ringed hand holding
a vase. The rose-shaped stopper is meant to symbolize the perfume. The design is painted in gold
and enamel. Emery-finished stopper.

CYCLAMEN, Elizabeth Arden, 1938.
Body of the bottle in white opal crystal with a gilded edge. Stopper and
foot in clear moulded and recut crystal, the foot heat-joined to the body.
Emery-finished stopper.

COQUE D'OR (Golden Bow), Guerlain, 1937.
Butterfly-shaped bottle in gilded cobalt-blue crystal. The inscription
is etched on the bottle. Emery-finished stopper.

Cream jug, c. 1855. Body in *pâte-de-riz* agate glass; *bleu céleste* agate glass handle, formed when hot in the shape of a snake.

Ornamental bottle, c. 1855. Two snakes in *bleu céleste* agate glass encircle the body and stopper made in *pâte-de-riz* agate glass.

Facing page: ornamental bottle, c. 1838. Clear crystal cased with cobalt-blue crystal.

Cream jug in *pâte-de-riz* agate glass, c. 1849. Three-cornered flame-opened lip; handle moulded, cut and heat-joined.

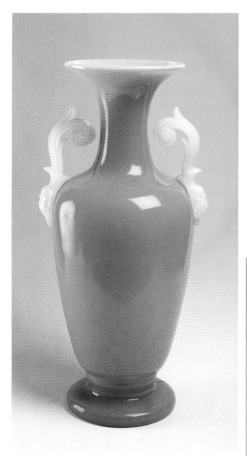

Vase, shown at the Exposition Nationale of 1849. In *pâte-de-riz* agate glass cased with *bleu céleste* agate, with handles moulded, cut and heat-joined. The judges praised this novel way of decorating an otherwise classically shaped vase.

Ornamental bottle, shown at the Exposition Universelle of 1855. In *pâte-de-riz* agate glass. The cabochons in *bleu céleste*, pink and chrysoprase-green agate glass have been cut, then heat-joined to the body.

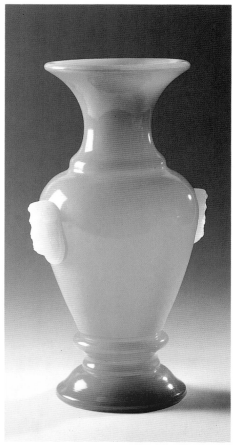

Vase, shown at the Exposition Nationale of 1849. *Pâte-de-riz* agate glass cased with pink agate. Two imitation-cameo mask-like faces are moulded on each side of the vase, a novel type of decoration commended by the exhibition jury as an important advance in crystal's 'war against porcelain'.

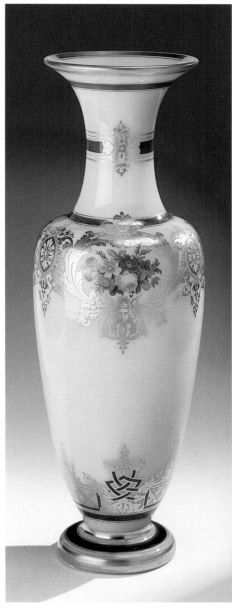

Vase, c. 1845–50. White opal crystal. The painted design, attributed to Jean-François Robert, in gold and multicoloured enamels, shows three bouquets of flowers in stylized scrolls and gilded motifs similar to those used on Beauvais upholstery fabrics or Sèvres porcelain of the same period.

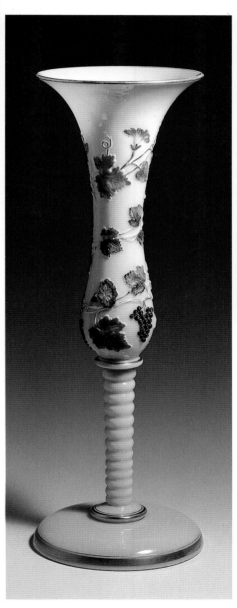

Vase, shown at the Exposition Universelle of 1855. In white opal crystal, it consists of three heat-joined sections. The blown bowl is flame-opened and bears an embossed torsade of gilded and multicoloured enamel morning glory flowers and vine leaves. The hollow stem has thirteen rings, formed with tongs, and two applied steps at the top and base. The foot is flame-opened in the shape of an inverted saucer.

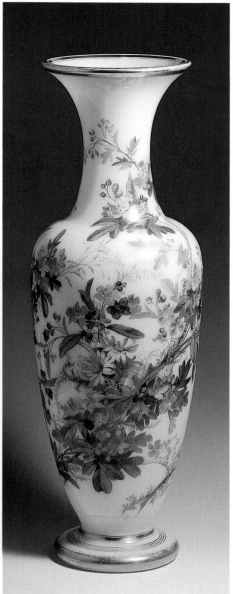

Vase, 1845–50. White opal crystal, with a floral design painted with multicoloured enamels and gold. Attributed to Jean-François Robert.

Page 218. DIORISSIMO, Christian Dior, 1955. The body of the bottle is decorated with flat cuts, as is the solid foot, which also bears a cut star and is set into a circle of gilded bronze. The crystal stopper is set inside a gilded bronze cap designed by the bronzeworker Charles. The cap shows the three flowers – rose, carnation and jasmine – upon which 'Diorissimo' perfume is based. This bottle, which is said to have been designed by Christian Dior himself, is inspired by a Louis XVI vase in porcelain and bronze.

219. V'E VERSACE, Gianni Versace, 1989. Designed by Thierry Lecoule. Baccarat made the glass case, but not the perfume bottle that fits inside it. Like the planet earth, the case leans slightly to one side of its central axis, the perfume bottle being wedged at its centre. The lid is hinged in such a way that the case can only be closed gently. The model in crystal was made in a limited edition of 90 copies.

223. Vase, shown at the Exposition Universelle of 1867. *Pâte-de-riz* agate glass cased with pink agate glass, with etched and gilded bacchanalian scenes and neo-Grecian motifs. A similar vase, cased with blue agate glass and decorated with a different set of figures (the chariot transporting Bacchus being drawn by two tigers rather than by deer), is in the Chrysler Museum in Norfolk, Virginia. Galerie Suger Collection, Paris.

224. Medici dish, on stand, shown at the Exposition Universelle of 1855. *Pâte-de-riz* agate glass and chrysoprase-green agate glass. The hand-painted decoration displays the shiny and mat effects of gilding partially burnished with an agate stone. The base, bowl and handles – composed of four snakes with drops of crimson crystal for eyes – have been heat-joined.

226. Towel-holder, shown at the Exposition in Nancy in 1909. The shape, previously used by Baccarat with a wheel-engraved design at the Exposition Universelle of 1878, is inspired by 16th-century reliquaries. The moulded stem with lions' heads is typical of Venetian glasswork of the same period. This model, in white opal crystal painted with multicoloured enamels, is decorated with a rustic scene in the style of 18th-century porcelain decorations.

227. Vase with lid, shown at the Exposition in Nancy in 1909. Inspired by a porcelain model from the 18th century, this vase in white opal crystal is painted with multicoloured enamels.

229. Study for a vase, made in December 1866, for the Exposition Universelle of 1867. Pencil drawing with watercolour and gouache on heavy paper.

Pair of vases, c. 1855. The floral design, painted with multicoloured enamels and gold on white opal crystal, is attributed to Jean-François Robert. Galerie Suger Collection, Paris.

Facing page: detail of the design.

Vase, c. 1855. White opal crystal painted with multicoloured enamels and gold, attributed to Jean-François Robert. Galerie Suger Collection, Paris.

Facing page: detail of the design.

Vase, 1854–55. White opal crystal cased with cobalt-blue crystal.
Baluster-shaped, with a rounded rim, decorated with flat cuts. Floral design
painted with multicoloured enamels and gold, attributed to Jean-François
Robert. Galerie Suger Collection, Paris.

Facing page: detail of the design.

Pair of large vases (height: 1.15 m/3 ft 7 in.), c. 1882. Each vase consists of three pieces in white opal crystal with a frame and base in Louis XVI-style gilded bronze. The romantic scenes in the style of 18th-century painting, signed E. Froger, are painted in monochrome enamel similar to the grisaille traditionally used for the painting of reliefs on stained-glass windows.

Facing page: large vase (height: 81 cm/2 ft 8 in.), one of a pair, Napoleon III era. The Medici-style basin and cylindrical stand, supported by an imposing Renaissance-style gilded bronze frame, are in white opal crystal painted with battle scenes and Napoleonic emblems.

B.Simon. Gvr à BACCARAT 1866.

Page 238. Detail of the right-hand vase on page 239: *L'Allégorie de la terre ou Cérès tenant Triptolème* (Allegory of Earth, or Ceres Holding Triptolemus) after a painting by Charles-Joseph Natoire (1700–77) executed for the château of Grimod du Fort in Orsay. A painter of romantic scenes and friend of Boucher, Natoire was famous for his decoration of the Queen's bedroom at Versailles in 1734, which won him an excellent reputation for interior decorating among the court nobility before he departed for Rome to direct the French Academy there. This allegory, part of a series of four (water, earth, air and fire), was engraved in reverse in an oval composition by J.-B. Perronneau. It was this engraving that served as the model for Jean-Baptiste Simon, who transposed it into a wheel-engraving on crystal, this time the same way round as Natoire's original painting. Ceres, daughter of Cronos and goddess of wheat, chose Prince Triptolemus as her ambassador among men, teaching him how to grow and harvest wheat. One of the episodes of the myth describes how she nurses the young baby and anoints him daily with ambrosia so that he will remain eternally young.

239 (left). ALLÉGORIE DE L'EAU (Allegory of Water): vase with lid, one of a pair, in clear crystal cased with crimson crystal, in three pieces (foot, bowl and lid) supported by a silver-plated bronze stand and inner threading. Signed and dated J.-B. Simon, engraver at Baccarat, 1867.
The two lidded vases, and the large serving bowl (page 71), were engraved by Jean-Baptiste Simon in 1866–67 and shown at the Exposition Universelle of 1867. Symbolizing Water and greatly influenced by Renaissance art, the left-hand vase bears an oval medallion reproducing the painting by Charles-Joseph Natoire *L'Eau ou Le Triomphe d'Amphitrite* (Water, or the Triumph of Amphitrite). The painting was engraved in reverse in an oval composition by P. Aveline. Simon made use of a print of this on paper, again transposing it so that it was the same way round as the original. Amphitrite, goddess of the sea and wife of Poseidon, is carried by two dolphins, with her son Triton and Nereids at her side. On the opposite side of the vase is a portrait of Poseidon. Above the shoulder of the vase, freshwater creatures – crayfish, otter, frog and snake – are intertwined in a scroll of acanthus leaves. At the base, groups of fish and crustaceans hang down from mask-like faces.

239 (right). ALLÉGORIE DE LA TERRE (Allegory of Earth): vase with lid engraved by Jean-Baptiste Simon in 1866. Various earthly fruits are used here to define the element Earth. On the side shown is the medallion inspired by Natoire's painting of Ceres, the wheat goddess. On the opposite side is a portrait of Cybele, goddess of fertility. Above the shoulder of the vase, a scroll of acanthus leaves houses animals of the forest. On the base, groups of fruit are suspended from mask-like faces.

240. Detail of the left-hand vase on page 239: the sea-horses, grotesque mask and plant scrolls derived from Renaissance motifs seem to have been reworked in the style of 18th-century decorative designs by the Bérain family.

241. Detail of one of the stands in chased silver-plated bronze which support the two vases engraved by Jean-Baptiste Simon in 1866–67 (page 239). Four finely chiselled masks, two masculine and two feminine, capped with upright scallop-shells, are placed at each of the four angles of the stand. These masks are reminiscent of Renaissance bronze motifs as revived by such early-19th-century artists as Barye, Feuchère and Chenavard.

243. Study of a vase, January 1863. Pencil drawing with watercolour and gouache on heavy paper.

244. LES TROIS GRACES (The Three Graces), 1906. In crystal and gilded bronze after a composition by François Moreau (born Dijon, 1832), inspired by Etienne Falconnet's 'Three Graces' clock (late 18th century). The theme of the Three Graces was frequently used for interior sculptures. Here it has been adapted to the canons of Art Nouveau.

245. Study for a vase with a bronze setting, c. 1865. Pencil drawing with watercolour and gouache on heavy paper.

246. Vase, shown at the Exposition Universelle of 1867. It has the shape of an ancient Greek crater, although here the handles have been applied to the clear crystal and formed when hot. The design is made by silver cementation, which gives the crystal a superficial amber colour after annealing. The blocked-out background of the motifs, the half-tone effects and the satin finish represent the most refined and elaborate etching techniques. The gilding for the handles and threads has been applied by hand. For the Exposition Universelle of 1867 Baccarat prepared a series of vases based on the cult of Bacchus, using neo-classical figurative motifs inspired by antique bas-reliefs in the style of the Borghese vase in the Louvre. A combination of all the figures was etched on a large punch bowl in clear crystal cased with blue crystal, now in the Corning Museum of Glass, New York. Private collection.

247. Detail of the vase on page 246. Stylized scrolls surround a cymbal-player wearing a lion skin in celebration of the cult of Bacchus, 1867.

248. Anthemia vase, 1902. The Chinese shape, created in 1878, is employed here with an etched anthemia design on clear crystal cased with pink crystal. Private collection.

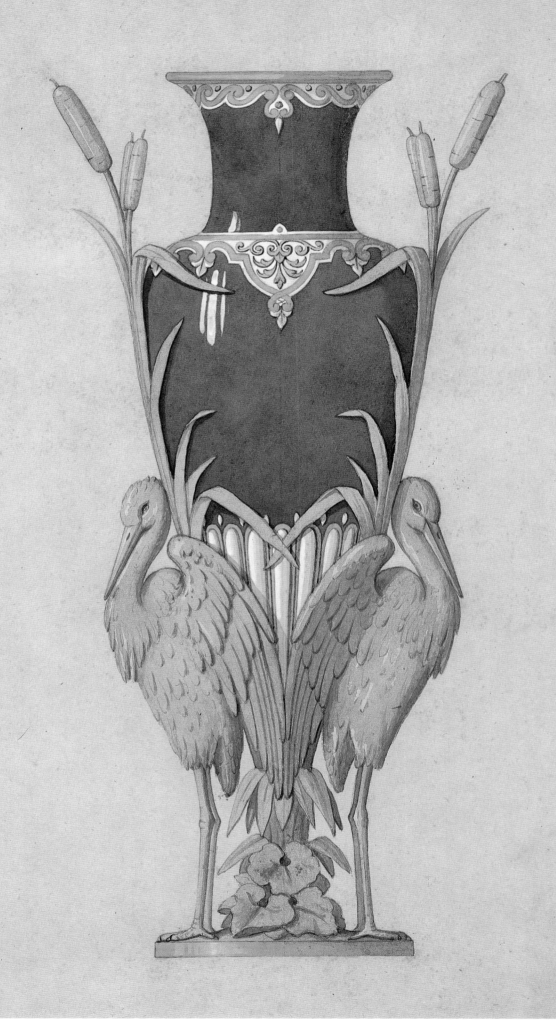

Vase with roses, late 19th century.
Light blue crystal cased with white
opal crystal. The design is etched and
painted with multicoloured enamels
and gold.

Vase with irises, 1900. Moss-coloured
crystal cased with pink crystal, etched
and gilded.

Vase with dahlias, late 19th century.
Light blue crystal cased with white
opal crystal, etched and painted with
another rare design in multicoloured
enamels and gold.

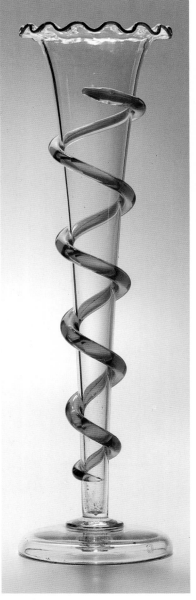

Vase by André Ballet, c. 1924. André Ballet's work for Baccarat used light decorative motifs that were painted with multicoloured opaque enamels or wheel-engraved, as on this vase.

Vase, mid-19th century, Conically shaped, with a blown foot, it is decorated with a pink crystal snake and a scalloped pink edge that has been flame-opened.

Vase with fish, shown at the Exposition Universelle of 1878. Part of a Japanese-influenced series of pieces with intaglio designs and acid polishing, inspired by 18th- and 19th-century engravings by Hokusai and Hiroshige. The international exhibitions of London in 1862 and Paris in 1867 introduced Japanese art to the West and it became a rich source of inspiration for European artists.

Facing page: vase, exhibited at the Exposition Universelle of 1878. Wheel-engraved design. The shape is derived from German stoneware, which had already served as the model for pieces of Sèvres porcelain, made from drawings by Aimé Chenavard in c. 1835.

Square anthemia vase, 1900. Clear
crystal cased with pink crystal; etched
design. Private collection.

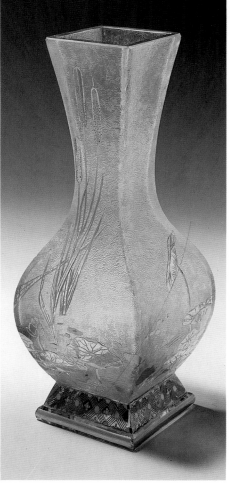

Vase, 1887. Japanese-influenced
design, consisting of bamboos carved
in intaglio and gilded. The stand is
made up of oak leaves and acorns in
moulded, cut and gilded bronze.

Vase with waterlilies and reeds, 1896.
Inspired by Chinese shapes and
motifs, this vase is etched and gilded.

Vase, c. 1885. Moulded crystal with twisted stylized bamboos. Plant motifs painted in opaque enamel and gold, with gilded brass embellishments.

Single-flower vase with tiger lily, 1898. Moss-coloured crystal cased with pink crystal, flame-opened and scalloped. The design is etched and gilded, and the pedestal, imitating branches, is in gilded bronze.

Vase, 1910. Cylindrical shape in triple-cased crystal (clear, white opal and pink)
with a richly cut design.

Vase, c. 1908. Cylindrical shape in triple-cased crystal (clear, white opal and blue).
Part of a series of experiments using etching techniques to print six different photographs
on triple-cased crystal surfaces.

Facing page: vase, c. 1924. Black crystal formed by turn-mould blowing.
The Chinese- or Japanese-inspired design was made with stencils and sand-cast engraving
and finished with a multicoloured lustre glaze.

FEMME DANS UN HAMAC (Woman in a Hammock), ice bucket, 1929. Wheel-engraving from a design by Georges Chevalier.

Facing page: VECTEUR (Vector) vase, designed by Nicolas Triboulot, 1990. The two sections interlock. The stand is in solid clear crystal, and the triangular vase is in cobalt-blue crystal.

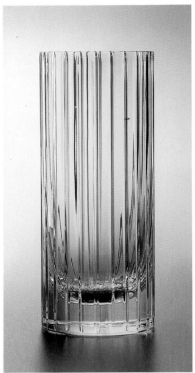

HARMONIE (Harmony) vase,
1975. Crystal cut with
vertical bezels.

Vase, 1949. Crystal cut with
deep bezels. Heavy, stable
and luminous vases of this
type came into vogue at the
end of the 1940s.

Vase, 1930. Thick, heavy crystal, cut in the
shape of a cylindrical gearwheel. The
tendency to link the arts to industrial
production arose after the Exposition des
Arts Décoratifs in 1925. In 1929 the Union
des Artistes Modernes (UAM) was founded,
with such leading members as Le Corbusier
and Jean Puiforcat. Close in spirit to the
UAM movement, which favoured form over
decoration, this vase is an extraordinary
example of the interplay of the artistic and
industrial worlds.

ANGLES vases, designed by Roberto Sambonet, 1975. This series of four vases, identically proportioned but in different heights, could be assembled, according to Sambonet, to create 'a suggestive and mathematically inevitable interplay' of shapes.

Square bowl in turquoise-blue crystal, 1884. The swallows are painted
in opaque enamels and gold. Gilded bronze mount.

Large bowl in amber-coloured crystal, 1890. Etched and gilded design of
leaves and branches. The gilded bronze stand is moulded and chiselled
with oak leaves and acorns. Private collection.

Vase with poinsettia, 1899. This model, with its Chinese-style shape, was first shown at the
Exposition Universelle of 1878 in a wheel-engraved version. Here the moss-coloured crystal cased
with amethyst crystal has been etched and retouched with gold brushwork. The mount is in silver.

Dish, c. 1865. White opal crystal, decorated with blue enamel. The stand is in gilded brass.

Bowl, c. 1865. White opal crystal, painted with a pastoral scene with birds. The mount is in gilded bronze. Galerie Suger Collection, Paris.

Detail: heron-like bird painted in multicoloured enamels on the white opal crystal.

Vase with foot, one of a pair, 1864. White opal crystal, with a pastoral scene with
a pheasant, painted in multicoloured enamels. Galerie Suger Collection, Paris.

Bowl, 1863. The crystal is etched with a fishing scene. The mount is in gilded bronze.
Private collection.

Overleaf: CASTOR ET POLLUX (Castor and Pollux), designed by Salvador Dalí, 1975. In 500 numbered pairs. 'In the beginning, man was torn apart; cutting himself in half, he reproduced himself by parthenogenesis. These architectural structures are a perfect representation of the dividing of the androgynous being at the moment he tears himself in half' (Dalí).

AILERON DE REQUIN (Shark's Fin), designed by Roberto Sambonet, 1982. Baccarat produced
a series of marine-inspired models by this Italian designer between 1972 and 1982.

Facing page: L'OIE ZOÉ (Zoë the Goose). Part of Baccarat's 'Fabulous Bestiary' series made from
blocks of burin-cut crystal, then decorated with silver, silver gilt and semi-precious stones by
the jeweller Chaumet; 41 copies made in 1972, 32 others in 1980.

LIÈVRE (Hare), bas-relief, one of a series of four (bull, horse, bear and hare),
designed by Bernard Augst, 1976. Each model was issued in 60 copies using
the lost-wax process.

MARATHON, decorative block, one of a series of six, made in 1987,
reproducing drawings by the painter Ung-No Lee using sand-cast engraving.

Small clock, designed in 1924 and shown at the Exposition Internationale des Arts Décoratifs in 1925. The bas-relief design has been moulded, frosted and cut. Reissued in 1989.

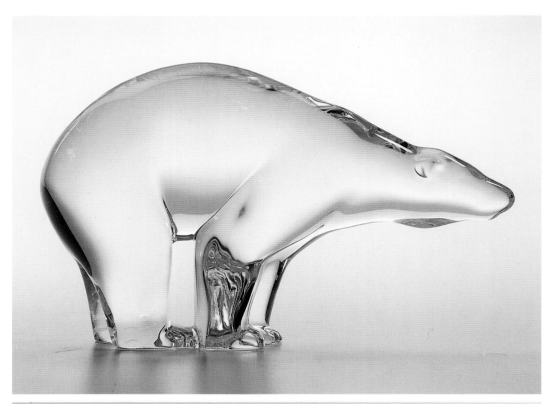

Ours Polaire (Polar Bear), designed by Georges Chevalier, 1929. Reissued in 1975.

Chatte (She-Cat), designed by Bernard Augst, 1987. In two versions: clear crystal and black crystal.

MOUFLON (Wild Sheep), designed by Bernard Georgeon, head of Baccarat's design department in 1975; twelve copies made using the lost-wax process.

TENSION, designed by Thomas Bastide, 1990. The crystal is cased on one side only with cobalt-blue crystal and the colour is projected on to the stand. Symbolizing night and day and the passing of time, the two pieces interlock in varying positions.

Facing page: ENERGY TRANSFORMED, designed by Bijan Bahar, 1980. In a limited edition of 25 copies.

Overleaf: DIVA, vase designed by Nicolas Triboulet, 1990.

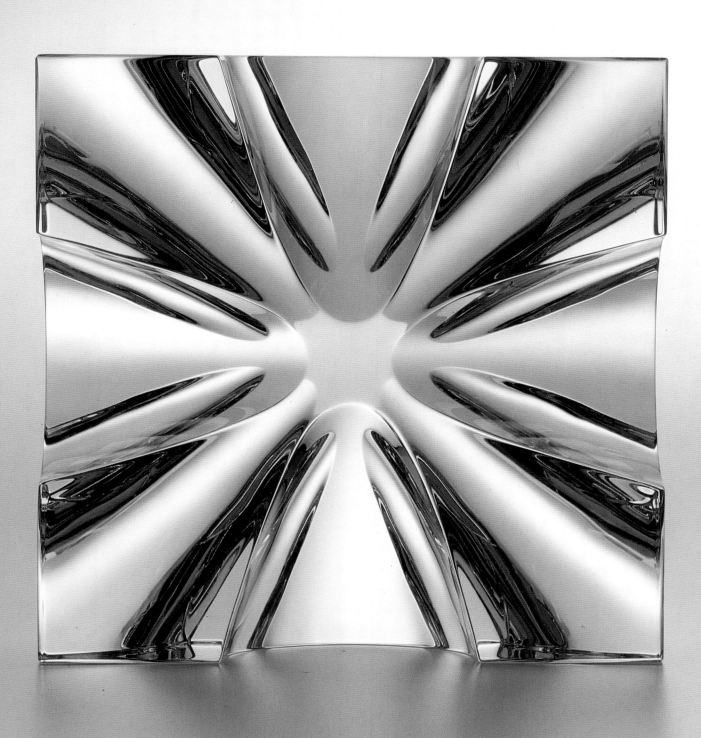

Régence-style chandelier, shown at the Exposition in Nancy in 1909. In cut crystal and moulded, chiselled and gilded bronze, with 31 electric bulbs. Height: 1.4 m/4 ft 6 in.

A table setting, in one of the warehouse exhibition halls, c. 1935. The decanters are from the DAVOS service (1930) and the water jugs from the POUR LE YACHT (For the Yacht) service (1925). Original photograph on glass plate.

Overleaf: design for a fountain.

GLOSSARY

AGATE GLASS: a translucent or semi-opaque glass with a silica, potassium, lime and lime phosphate base. The fusion of these materials produces a suspension of micro-bubbles and micro-crystals within the vitreous mass, with resulting opacification. The melting point of agate is higher than that of crystal because agate contains a high proportion of silica but no lead. Because it is particularly hard, agate is rarely cut. When white, it is known as *pâte-de-riz*. It can be coloured by the addition of metallic oxides. In the nineteenth century, certain colours had specific names: *bleu céleste* or 'celestial blue' for copper oxide, 'chrysoprase green' for copper and uranium oxides (uranium oxide has since been replaced by vanadium oxide). A pink shade is obtained with colloidal gold or with tin and antimony oxides.

This type of glass was discovered in sixteenth-century Venice and reproduced in 1837 by one of the Count of Buquoy's glassworks in Georgenthal in Bohemia. François-Eugène de Fontenay began producing it at Baccarat in 1842. The rounded shapes and bright colours with which it tended to be associated were especially appreciated during the Romantic era, and agate glass remained in fashion until 1870.

ANNEALING: the toughening of glass by heating and slow cooling. Also the heating of crystal in order to fix laid-on colours.

APPLIED CRYSTAL: molten crystal added in varying amounts to the object being made (to form, for example, a foot, a handle or some kind of embellishment).

BLOWING: a technique of shaping a crystal object by using blown air.
1. Turn-mould blowing: held at the end of a blowpipe, the crystal 'parison' is placed into a mould, where it is blown, so that the crystal adheres to the sides of the mould, and then turned rapidly to eliminate the traces of the mould's seams and make the surface perfectly smooth.
2. Hot-mould blowing: the 'parison', at the end of a blowpipe, is put into a mould and forced against the sides of the mould by means of air pressure.

BLOWPIPE: a hollow metal rod used to gather up a ball of molten crystal, which is then shaped by blowing.

BOWL: formed by blowing, the upper part of a glass intended to hold liquids. In a wine service, the bowls of the various glasses are usually identically proportioned, with the exception of flute glasses, champagne glasses, hock glasses and other glasses with an idiosyncratic shape. There are seven main types of bowl: balloon, funnel-shaped, tulip-shaped, conical, cylindrical, egg-shaped and saucer-shaped. Burgundy wines are best drunk from balloon shapes, whose wider bowl gives the aroma a chance to develop (the Masséna service). Funnel-shaped bowls are best for claret, which needs depth so that the tannin can sink to the bottom (the Harcourt service). The tulip shape either takes its inspiration from the Italian Renaissance (the Vallée service) or is in the form of a bell (the Beaune service). Whatever shape a wine service may have, each glass's size or shape corresponds to a specific function.

CASED CRYSTAL: two layers of differently coloured crystal overlaid while the crystal is still hot. In general, one of the layers is clear, the other coloured (see CRYSTAL COLOURS). Casing is particularly effective when used on objects which have been cut or engraved so that one of the colours is partially revealed.

CEMENTATION: a process for tinting the upper layer of crystal by means of a paste compound consisting of a clay or ferrous oxide support and a silver salt. After firing and elimination of the paste, the surface is tinted an amber-yellow colour. A systematic study of this phenomenon was undertaken in around 1874 by a certain P. Ebell, who introduced the term cementation by analogy with the cementation of carburized steel. The process was already in use at Baccarat in the early 1860s, as well as on pieces shown at the Exposition Universelle of 1867. A similar process using copper obtained a red shade on vitreous surfaces.

CRYSTAL COLOURS: crystal colours are made by adding metallic oxides to the melt. A vast palette of shades can be obtained by varying the proportions of metallic oxide or by combining them. Two colouration techniques exist: ionic and colloidal. Ionic colourations are due to the presence of metallic ions in the crystal and occur at the moment the melting point is reached. The principal ionic colourations are blue obtained with cobalt, green with chrome, amethyst with manganese, turquoise with copper, etc. Colloidal colours are obtained when the already formed object is gradually reheated in the taphole of a melting pot or in the furnace. This operation precipitates the metallic ions in the form of microparticles within the crystal. The resulting colouration is due to the diffusion of light by these microparticles. The colours obtained, which vary according to the length of time and intensity of the reheating operation, are reddish-pink obtained via gold, orange-yellow via gold and silver, and amethyst via gold and cobalt.

CULLET: pieces of good-quality crystal which are recycled with the raw materials during the melting process. The cullet consists of pieces of unused crystal: the surplus from blown or moulded objects, fragments from discarded items, crystal remaining in the melting pots, etc. Adding cullet to the melt reduces the amounts of raw materials needed and helps to speed up the melting process.

CUTTING (of crystal): a process of decorating crystal by tooling its surface with diamond-encrusted wheels or wheels made of iron, natural stone (sandstone) or artificial stone (Carborundum). The motifs produced in this manner have special names according to their shape and depth: bezels, flat cuts, punties, diamonds, olives, bamboos, etc.

DISCHARGE MOULD: a kind of container located at the end of a pump used to remove crystal from the melting pot.

EMERY FINISH: the finish produced by an operation in which the cone-shaped plug of a bottle stopper is ground down with fine emery powder. The stopper and its bottle are then engraved with the same number to ensure that they are not separated. This type of stoppering is completely airtight and can be used for highly volatile substances.

ENAMEL: glass which has been coloured at a very low melting point. It is applied to cold crystal objects and fixed by heating. At the application stage, enamel is a paste consisting of a fusible base that has been coloured with metallic oxides and pulverized to a fine powder, combined with an organic liquid (or binder) which allows it to be applied with a brush or transferred by silk-screen. Enamels are more or less thick depending on the dilution of the paste. After firing, they can be transparent or opaque depending on the composition of the fusible base. Widely used during the Middle Ages and the Renaissance, enamel decoration has been in fashion at various moments of recent history. At Baccarat, it was used in around 1843 by Jean-

François Robert, a painter and enameller on opaline. Following the precedent set in 1867 by Philippe-Joseph Brocard's reproductions of the opaque and embossed enamels used on Islamic glasswork, Baccarat exhibited enamelled decorations inspired by Japanese art, Art Nouveau and Art Deco from the Exposition Universelle of 1878 until around 1925.

ETCHING: a chemical technique for engraving glass and crystal by means of different sorts of acid baths with bases of sulphuric acid, hydrofluoric acid or fluorides. Certain acid baths have the effect of hollow etching the crystal to a depth proportionate to the length of time the crystal remains in contact with the bath, resulting in a shiny surface. Other acid baths of varying compositions create a mat finish, while yet others give a bright lustre to frosted crystal. Certain baths are combined successively to produce an etching that is both hollow and frosted, referred to as 'Venetian engraving'. The capacity of hydrofluoric acid (a combination of fluorite and sulphuric acid) to attack glass was first discovered in the seventeenth century. The process was applied industrially from 1855, when the chemist L. Kessler succeeded in producing large quantities of the acid that were both economical and harmless. In 1854 Kessler had invented the printing and transfer process by means of reserved areas of decoration on ink-coated surfaces. This process could be used in series on pieces of all different sizes and shapes. Originally, these reserved patterns were printed on paper using lithographic techniques, that is, by means of limestones etched with acid. The stones were soon replaced by sheets of etched steel, which, though more costly, produced finer designs. From 1856 to 1867 Baccarat purchased its acid supplies exclusively from Kessler. But it was not until 1864, when it acquired the frosted acid etching process, that Baccarat began to make full use of etching techniques.

ETCHING (ARAB): another process using acid baths. The object is coated with a layer of wax and the design is then drawn in the wax using an etching needle. The needle is guided by the rotation of a toothed wheel adjusted to produce the desired motifs. Each machine can draw the same motif simultaneously on twelve glasses. Arab etching, which appeared in around 1885, takes its name from the motifs it produces, which resemble arabesques. In 1889, when the fashion for this type of decoration was at its height, there were twelve such machines at Baccarat.

FERRET: the solid metal rod used to remove small quantities of molten crystal from the melting pot.

FLUX: substance added in glassmaking to promote vitrification.

FROSTED: the term used of a glass surface which, being slightly rough or uneven, lacks its usual transparency and brilliance, presenting instead a more or less pronounced mat aspect due to the way it diffuses light. A surface of this type is made by an acid bath, by sanding, or by the action of a grinding wheel.

GILDED EMBOSSED DESIGN: a gilded design in relief applied to a decorative motif that has been painted a certain thickness with an opaque enamel. The technique was exhibited by the Bavarian glassworks of Schachtenbach at the Exposition Universelle prior to 1855. Over the next few years Baccarat experimented with ways of reproducing the technique, but it is probable that Jean-François Robert had already used it on enamelled opalines in 1855. The technique was used extensively at Baccarat in around 1878 and 1909.

GILDING: a decorating process consisting of painting crystal with a brush dipped in a gold-based paste made of vitreous flux combined with an organic binding material. Powdered gold can be added to enhance the gilding. Another method of application uses a silk-screen process. A thermal cycle is necessary to fix the gold on the crystal by means of the vitreous flux. Certain golds have a shiny appearance after being heated; others have a mat finish and can be burnished with a hard stone (agate or bloodstone). Gilding was already in use at Baccarat in 1833.

HEAT-JOINING: a technique for assembling two pieces of crystal so as to form a single object (for example, the stem and bowl of a glass). Joining is done either while the object is being formed at a high temperature, or by reheating and partially melting the specific areas that are to be joined (without deforming the object in the process). Unlike crystal pieces that are joined directly, with heat-joining the two pieces to be joined are subjected to an increase in temperature.

HOCK (or RHINE WINE) GLASS: a glass whose bowl is usually tinted, following the tradition of masking the colours of Rhine wines. Nineteenth-century German glassmakers and their imitators used hollow stems, but since the beginning of this century hock glasses have been made with tall, solid stems.

HOT WORKSHOP: the building which houses one or more furnaces and where the glassmakers work. There are currently four hot workshops at Baccarat.

INTAGLIO: a process of ornamentation which gives a result somewhere between engraving and cutting. Using small corundum wheels that are larger than engraving wheels, the intaglio process hollows the crystal to varying depths, leaving a mat imprint which can subsequently be polished by means of an acid bath. This method was used extensively at Baccarat in around 1878 and at the beginning of the twentieth century.

KNOP: a rounded protuberance formed when hot. Often cut, it is used to decorate glass stems.

LUSTRE GLAZE: a mineral-based varnish consisting of an organo-metallic fixing agent combined with mineral salts and applied to the surface of a glass or crystal object to colour it after firing. In contrast to enamel glazes, lustre glazes are always transparent and extremely thin. They often have an iridescent sheen. Lustre glazes are rarely used in crystalwork because of their poor adherence after firing, but they can be found at Baccarat on certain novelty pieces dating from 1880–85, in conjunction with enamel decorations, and on frosted pieces from the 1915–25 period.

METAL: the material used for making glass, especially in its molten state.

MILLEFIORI: a tightly compressed assemblage of sections of coloured crystal rods (or beads) encased in glass to create objects or decorative additions for objects: paperweights, bottles, vases, bowls, jewelry, etc. The word 'millefiori' comes from the Italian and suggests a 'carpet of flowers'. Discovered under the Roman Empire, the millefiori technique was successfully revived for the manufacturing of paperweights in the mid-nineteenth century. The first such item was shown by the Venetian glassmaker P. Bigaglia at the Exhibition of Austrian Industrial Products, held in Vienna in 1845. Baccarat began using the technique in 1846.

MOULDING: different techniques exist for moulding crystal. All require that the crystal be hot and, in contrast with blowing, none uses blown air.
1. Press-moulding: the crystal is poured into a mould and pressed against the sides by means of a core operated by a press. The core forms the base or hollow of a variety of objects: tumblers, bowls, and plates, in addition to heavier pieces. This technique was perfected in the United States and rapidly developed in France in around 1825, with the aim of reproducing cut-glass-type decorations less expensively. In around 1825 'sanded' motifs

were used to mask imperfections on the surface caused by the difference in temperature between the molten crystal and the mould. When subsequent technical improvements eliminated such side effects, press-moulding became a means of applying decorative motifs that were impossible to cut or etch, as well as serving to manufacture heavy objects, provided that they could be removed easily from the mould.

2. Injection moulding: the crystal contained in the discharge mould is injected into a mould by means of a piston.

3. Centrifugal moulding: centrifugal force is used to throw the crystal against the sides of a conical, one-piece mould.

4. Hot-forming: similar to the technique of lost-wax casting, this process involves pouring the crystal into a mould made of fireclay which is destroyed when the object is removed.

MOUSSELINE or MUSLIN CRYSTAL: an extremely thin crystal developed after 1850, generally used for luxury pieces.

OPAL CRYSTAL: a type of crystal that varies from the translucent to the opaque, and which can be milky white or coloured due to the presence of metallic oxides. Its opacity is obtained by adding opacifying agents to the crystal composition. The opacifying agents of opal are calcium phosphate (formerly obtained from calcified bones, producing reddish highlights by refraction of an intense white light), calcium fluoride and tin oxide. The term opal crystal, already employed in the eighteenth century, derives from the crystal's similarity to opal, a natural form of hydrated silica.

OPALINE: a generic term from the end of the nineteenth century referring to any glass or crystal object which has been opalized or opacified.

PARISON: a mass of crystal gathered on the end of a blowpipe and partially shaped by rolling before being blown.

PUNTY: 1. A solid metal rod, with or without a head, used to grip a heated crystal object. The imprint of the punty, usually at the base of the object, is removed when the object is cut.

2. By analogy, a roundel motif cut into a crystal surface.

RECUT: the light cutting of a crystal object whose preliminary shape or decoration has been obtained by moulding.

RIM: the upper part of a bowl, usually devoid of any decoration. The upper edge is rounded and can be fashioned by the glassmaker in several ways, either when the glass is hot, or when the glass is cold by means of a series of cuts followed by acid polishing, or by burning with a flame. This upper edge may eventually be painted with gold thread.

RING: a line of crystal of varying thickness applied horizontally on a usually rounded surface. On the neck of a jug the ring is both decorative and functional, since it provides the neck with a better grip and prevents the hand from slipping.

SATIN FINISH: a particularly refined and smooth finish on a frosted surface, generally obtained by a highly controlled use of acid, by means either of an acid bath that has been greatly diluted or of an extremely short immersion in an acid bath.

STEP: a small lip located at the base of the stem formed when the stem is drawn. The step can be left, or it can be reabsorbed when the foot is shaped. For purposes of symmetry, a supplementary step may be formed between the bowl and the stem.

SULPHIDE: 1. A motif made of ceramic paste that has been compressed and filtered at a high temperature, then encased in glass to produce an imitation of old-fashioned cameos engraved in hard stone. These motifs are often contained in crystal objects (paperweights, goblets, bottles, etc.) designed for commemorative occasions.

2. By extension, the ornamental glass paperweight that contains a sulphide. The origin of the term 'sulphide' is uncertain; it may derive from the fact that the first such motifs encased in glass gave an appearance of silver sulphide because of the thin layer of gas which remained between the crystal and the ceramic motif. The technique of encasing sulphides in glass, discovered in 1796, was practised by d'Artigues at the Vonêche crystalworks in around 1810–15 and perfected in 1818 by the ceramist Boudon de Saint-Amans (1774–1858) in collaboration with the Creusot crystalworks.

TEMPERATURE

ANNEALING TEMPERATURE of lustre glazing, gilding and enamelling on crystal: located at around 500°C (930°F), this is the temperature that must be reached to fix the decoration without deforming the object. The temperature varies according to the proportions and types of flux used.

MELTING POINT OF CRYSTAL: the temperature between 1,350°C and 1,450°C (c. 2,460°F and 2,640°F) at which the composition is maintained for several hours in order to obtain a molten, homogeneous mass without bubbles.

WORKING TEMPERATURE OF CRYSTAL: the temperature of crystal when it is modelled. A distinction is made between the gathering temperature, around 1,250°C (2,280°F), when the glassworker removes the crystal from the pot, and the working range – between 950°C and 650°C (1,750°F and 1,200°F) – corresponding to the state of viscosity of the crystal which enables it to be modelled.

WHEEL-ENGRAVING: a decoration technique using an assortment of small wheels which delicately groove the surface of the crystal and produce mat motifs of varying depths. These small wheels are made of copper and must receive a constant supply of grinding powder (either emery or diamond powder) diluted with oil of turpentine to attack the crystal. Small wheels made of lead are then used to polish the hollow, mat motifs. Baccarat adopted the process of wheel-engraving in 1839, following the arrival of an engraver from Bohemia, and developed its own school of engraving, producing such outstanding talents as Jean-Baptiste Simon and Pétremant.

WORKING (COLD): the various operations which the crystal undergoes after annealing has taken place.

WORKING (HOT): the modelling and annealing of the crystal in the hot workshop.

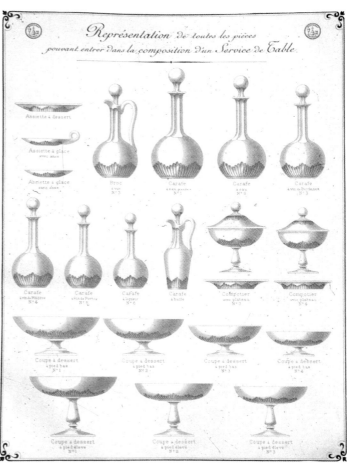

TRIPLE-CASED CRYSTAL: as cased crystal, but with three rather than two layers of different-coloured crystal overlaid. Even more layers of crystal may be cased, provided the compositions of the different layers are compatible.

WATER SET: a bedroom set consisting of four or five pieces on a matching tray – a large water carafe, a small carafe for orange-flower water, a sugar bowl, and one or two water glasses or tumblers. A simplified version of the water set consists of three matching pieces: a tray and a water carafe without a stopper, covered by an upturned tumbler.

Pages from a Baccarat catalogue illustrating a table service.

FACTORY MARKS AND SIGNATURES

Enamel applied by silk-screen,
c. 1865.

First version of the factory
mark: printed paper disk,
1862–1936.

Signature in relief on the mould,
dating from the late 1870s.

Etched or sanded mark,
after 1936.

Etched mark on perfume
bottles, c. 1920–30.

Laser-applied signature on
Baccarat creations from 1990,
extending progressively to the
entire Baccarat production.

Signature of Georges Chevalier,
either etched, wheel-engraved
or enamel-painted.

BIOGRAPHIES OF GLASS DESIGNERS

BERNARD AUGST (born in Francheville, 1934). Following in the footsteps of Georges Chevalier, Bernard Augst has continued the Baccarat bestiary since 1961, pursuing his early passion for sculpting animals. He has a particular gift for observing and capturing wild creatures in various typical attitudes – a great horned owl on a branch at dusk, a cat licking itself, a bull about to charge. An outstanding student at the Académie des Beaux-Arts in Rouen – he was first in France in painting (1955) and in sculpture (1956) – he later studied with Louis Leygue in Paris. Augst's multiple talents have been in demand for numerous monumental commissions in Paris, the provinces and Gabon, as well as for the renovation of historical buildings such as the Louvre and the Elysée palace. He took part in an exciting project to produce a facsimile of the Lascaux caves (1971–83) and since 1984 his sculptures have been commissioned for the French National Mint. Augst works mainly with wood and stone but has extended the range of his expertise by also experimenting with crystal. He avoids excessive ornamentation, concentrating on the essential and allowing the natural qualities of his materials full expression.

BIJAN BAHAR (born in Iran, 1942, a resident of the United States since 1959). The works of this sculptor and designer, a graduate of the California College of Arts and Crafts, have been exhibited in most of the large cities of America and are included in numerous private collections, including those of Farah Pahlavi, the former Empress of Iran; Mrs Louis B. Mayer, the wife of the founder of Metro-Goldwyn-Mayer; and the famous composer Quincy Jones. Convinced that the role of the artist is to create those things that nature is unable to create, Bijan Bahar opened his own art galleries in 1984, Gallery One in Beverly Hills and Gallery Two in New York, where he exhibits his own sculptures and those of young international artists. In 1980–81 he asked Baccarat to produce four massive geometrical blocks for an artistic experiment involving crystal and light.

ANDRÉ BALLET (born in Paris, 1885). André Ballet experimented in numerous areas of the applied arts – wallpaper, printed cloth, ceramics, cutlery, carpets, wrought-ironwork and book bindings. At the beginning of the 1920s he designed toiletry bottles for Louis Vuitton and a series of glasses, vases and bottles for Baccarat. These pieces were exhibited in 1923 at the Musée Galliera along with chandeliers, vases and bottles by Georges Chevalier and perfume bottles designed by Louis Süe (1875–1968) and André Mare (1885–1932), produced by Baccarat for the Orsay perfumery. The art magazine *Art et Décoration*, commenting on the exhibition, expressed its enthusiasm for André Ballet's decorations, painted 'with measured and delightful touches', in polychrome enamels in relief. These decorations were composed of precise and rhythmic arabesques and foliage, whose delicate style evoked Oriental calligraphy or seaweed floating on the ocean. In a similar vein, at the beginning of the 1930s, Ballet designed endpapers for collectors' books, creating decorative arabesques out of regular repetitions of numbers and monograms. Ballet's clients included Baron de Rothschild and Pope Pius XI.

GRAND DUC (Great Horned Owl), designed by Bernard Augst, 1980.

THOMAS BASTIDE (born in Biarritz, 1954). Upon completing his studies in graphic design and industrial art at the Ecole Penninghen and the Ecole des Arts Appliqués Olivier de Serre in Paris, Thomas Bastide worked for the Compagnie d'Esthétique Industrielle with the designer Raymond Loewy (1893–1986). After a year spent decorating the display windows of retailers throughout France for Baccarat and the porcelain manufacturer Bernardaud, in 1982 he joined Baccarat's design department. Bastide has designed numerous table settings and decorative objects. In recent years he has travelled regularly to the United States, attending the summer sessions devoted to glass designing at the Pilchuck School in Seattle, and taking part in promotional operations sponsored by Baccarat. In 1989 in Dallas, Texas, the National Tabletop Association awarded him a prize for his Neptune vases and bowls.

MILAN dish, designed by Thomas Bastide, 1990.

GEORGES CHEVALIER (born in Vitry-sur-Seine, 1894–1987). In the sixty-one years he worked at Baccarat (1916–76) Georges Chevalier designed so many different pieces, in so many different areas – chandeliers, bottles, table settings and decorative objects – that the exact number of his creations remains uncertain. His enormous influence on the production of crystal at Baccarat is nevertheless beyond doubt. As a student at the Ecole Nationale Supérieure des Arts Décoratifs in Paris, he became interested in architecture and design under the guidance of Maurice Dufrêne (1876–1955). Working for Léon Bakst (1866–1924), he participated from 1918 to 1924 in the creation of scenery and costumes for the Ballets Russes. The influence of this world-famous designer had a profound effect on Chevalier's work, as much by his choice of warm, bright colours as by his evocations of dancers and the sea. During the main period of his influence at Baccarat, Chevalier focused on crystal primarily as a source of transparency and purity. Until 1925 he also pursued his penchant for colours, using semi-figurative motifs painted in relief with polychrome enamels on functional, simply shaped objects. Gradually, however, Chevalier became aware of the specific qualities and requirements of crystal, and began to reason less as a painter and more as a sculptor, designing a bestiary between 1924 and 1930

SAINT-EXUPÉRY ink well, designed by Georges Chevalier, 1924. Reissued in 1989.

that employed the techniques of bas-relief. These first purely decorative pieces earned him the recognition of critics and art magazines. For the Exposition Internationale des Arts Décoratifs in 1925, Chevalier displayed the full range of his talents and his formidable energy, not only in the pieces he designed for Baccarat, but in the porcelain statuettes and clocks he created for La Maîtrise, Galeries Lafayette's design workshop, founded by Maurice Dufrêne after the First World War. In addition, collaborating with the designers René Joubert and Léon Albert Jallot, he created a dining room and man's bedroom suite for the French Embassy, and it was Chevalier who designed the Baccarat-Christofle pavilion for the Exposition Internationale des Arts Décoratifs in 1925, when he was selected as a member of the Glassware jury. Over the following years he exhibited annually at the Salon des Artistes Décorateurs. What strikes us today about Chevalier's creations for Baccarat, in particular the tableware and large decorative pieces, is not just their grace and beauty, but the technical difficulties they must have presented to the glassmakers – difficulties which, far from being circumvented to the detriment of the artist's ideas, were confronted, resolved and even

Gilded and enamelled dish, designed by Georges Chevalier, 1924.

transcended. Chevalier's preliminary drawings were in fact marked with precise instructions to the glassworkers and glass-cutters regarding the manufacturing procedures they were to follow. By discovering solutions to each of the manual and technical problems posed by his designs, he was able to involve hundreds of workers and technicians in his experiments with crystal.

Paperweight with sulphide of Theodore Roosevelt, sculpted by Albert David, 1965.

LE ROI SOLEIL (The Sun King), perfume bottle designed by Salvador Dalí for Elsa Schiaparelli, 1945.

SALVADOR DALÍ (born in Figueras, Catalonia, 1904–89). Baccarat made two objects from the Surrealist painter's designs. The first was a perfume bottle designed by Dalí in 1945 for his friend the clothes designer Elsa Schiaparelli. Called *Le Roy Soleil* (The Sun King), it represents an anthropomorphic figure symbolizing the sun setting over the ocean. The model was made from blown, moulded, cut, enamelled and gilded crystal in 3,012 copies in 1945 and 1946. Thirty years later Baccarat produced *Castor et Pollux* (Castor and Pollux), symbols of one of Dalí's favourite themes, the self-reproduction of the androgyne.

ALBERT DAVID (born in Liernais, Côte d'Or, 1896–1971). The career of the sculptor Albert David evolved along almost classical lines. A student of Jean Boucher at the Ecole des Beaux-Arts in Paris, he designed a number of monuments commemorating the dead of the First World War. His ceramic and bas-relief sculp-

tures were exhibited at the Salon des Artistes Français, the Salon d'Automne and the Salon des Artistes Décorateurs. After receiving an honourable mention in 1921, at the Exposition Universelle of 1937 he was awarded the Gold Medal. Named Chevalier of the Legion of Honour in 1938, he became one of the sculptors for the National Mint. As in the case of the sculptor and ironwork artist Gilbert Poillerat, sculpting for the Mint led naturally to making cameos for crystal paperweights. (The sulphides encased inside crystal were in fact the ceramic versions, in identical proportions, of prototypes sculpted in plaster of Paris or clay.) From 1959 to 1971 David sculpted ten portraits, including those of Pope Pius XII and Pope John XXIII as well as the American presidents John F. Kennedy, Theodore Roosevelt and Herbert Hoover.

FRANÇOIS-EUGÈNE DE FONTENAY (born in Autun, 1810–84). François-Eugène de Fontenay was one of those rare engineers with a passion for glassware who, between 1835 and 1845, were responsible for reviving colouring and decorating techniques that had fallen into disuse in France, in some cases for centuries. By providing these techniques with a firm scientific basis, they were able to raise glassmaking to industrial levels. A first-class graduate of the Ecole Centrale des Arts et Manufactures – founded in Paris in 1829 to further the development of the textile industry – Fontenay took over the direction of the Plaine-de-Walsch glassworks, in the Meurthe region, in 1832. Spurred on by the Société d'Encouragement pour l'Industrie Française, in collaboration with Jean-François Robert he perfected the technique of decorating glassware with vitrifiable colours (enamels). And in collaboration with Georges Bontemps (1799–1884), director of the glass factory and crystalworks of Choisy-le-Roi, he developed the technique

Bowl with foot in *pâte-de-riz* and chrysoprase-green agate glass, c. 1844.

of colouration by casing, or overlaying. The progress made by the Plaine-de-Walsch glassworks under Fontenay's expert direction inspired its owner, Baron de Klinglin, to found a second glassworks in Wallérysthal in 1838. Fontenay took charge of both establishments until 1841, when he accepted the offer of Baccarat's director, Jean-Baptiste Toussaint, to become second in charge at Baccarat. When Toussaint became manager in 1849, Fontenay took over the direction of the factory, a position he retained until 1871. In addition to developing techniques for colouring and decorating glass and crystal, he is also to be credited with regulating the duration of the melting process – and, consequently, regularizing the glassmakers' work schedule. He developed 'agate' glass, discovered how to obtain dichroic (crystal) colours from a uranium oxide base, and perfected the techniques for obtaining uniformly transparent glass and crystal. These achievements were technical milestones that enabled the glass industry to emerge as an authentic medium of artistic creation at the end of the nineteenth century.

THIERRY LECOULE (born in Frontignan, Hérault, 1954). After completing his studies in technical drawing, Thierry Lecoule worked in the planning department of the Masnières glassworks, the bottling branch of the BSN group. Involved in designing models, he began working with glass and became increasingly interested in it as a medium of artistic expression. It was for this reason that, in 1981, he went to work with the designer Alain de Mourgues in Paris. In 1985 he founded his own design studio and in 1990 he learned how to blow and model glass at the Sars-Poteries workshop in the north of France. He has

designed bottles for such perfumes as Grès, Régine's and Gianni Versace. His *V'e Versace* perfume bottle and case won him several prizes, including the Grand Prix de la Création de la Ville de Paris in 1989. As a designer of various lines of cosmetic products for the major perfume companies, he is interested in finding complementary motifs that express his commitment to each client. His interests also extend to other areas of design, including tableware, which he has again designed for Baccarat. His creations combine elegance and a mysterious quality of movement, appearing different from every angle.

UNG-NO LEE (1904–89). Ung-No Lee was born in Korea, the meeting place of traditional Japanese and Chinese cultures. Pursuing his passion for drawing and painting, he devoted twenty years to studying the graphic arts, becoming a professor at the University of Hong-Ik in Seoul. Ung-No Lee was thus an accomplished artist and teacher when he arrived in Paris in 1958 to found the Académie

EQUITATION (Horsemanship), sand-cast engraved crystal block after a drawing by Ung-No Lee, 1986.

de Peinture Orientale. Refusing to learn French, he relied solely on his teaching ability to make a success of the venture. His paintings in Indian ink and ink wash, inspired by the ancient art of Oriental calligraphy, were purchased by the Museum of Modern Art in Rome and the Museum of Modern Art in New York as well as by the Mobilier National and the Musée Cernuschi in Paris. Some of his designs have also been used on tapestries and pottery. Ung-No Lee was a poet as well as a painter and in his work he used the steady flow of animals or people, moving with rhythmic fluidity across the page, to express the complex messages of modern sociology. Six such 'ideograms' based on the Olympic sports, painted in black ink on paper in 1986, were engraved on blocks of crystal by Baccarat.

GILBERT POILLERAT (born in Mer, Loire-et-Cher, 1902–89). Gilbert Poillerat was an engraver, painter, sculptor and jewelry designer (for the clothes designer Jacques Heim), known above all for his metalwork. A graduate of the Ecole Boulle in Paris, he made

Paperweight with sulphide of the Marquis de La Fayette, sculpted by Gilbert Poillerat, 1955.

iron and bronze into mirrors, furniture and chandeliers, often using the theme of the sun as his point of departure. His profoundly classical art revived the tradition of baroque metalwork in the style of the grilles of Place Stanislas in Nancy. After the Second World War he received several official commissions to design grilles for the Eiffel Tower, the Louvre, ocean liners and the presidential suites at the Elysée palace as well as at Rambouillet and Marly. Appointed professor at the Ecole Nationale Supérieure des Arts Décoratifs in 1947, he also engraved medals for the National Mint. It was this activity which led Poillerat to sculpt prototypes for sulphides. He was the first sculptor to be taken on in 1952–53 when Baccarat decided to relaunch its paperweights. By 1955 Poillerat had designed twelve prototypes, including portraits of the Marquis de La Fayette and Queen Elizabeth II, as well as the twelve signs of the Zodiac based on drawings by Raphael.

ROBERT RIGOT (born in Buxy, Saône-et-Loire, 1929). Robert Rigot still lives in the little

Burgundian village where he was born, and where his father taught him to sculpt in stone. In 1954, as a student at the Académie des Beaux-Arts in Paris, Rigot won the Grand Prix de Rome and he spent four years at the French Academy in the Villa Medici in Rome, concentrating on bronzework. On his return to France he received numerous commissions for ornamental work in high schools and municipal buildings built during the 1960s. His sculptures in bronze, often of birds and insects, combine generous, rounded or structured shapes with paradoxically rough, jagged surfaces. In 1968 Baccarat proposed that he work in a different medium which would allow him to experiment

LIBERTÉ AILÉE (Winged Liberty), designed by Robert Rigot, 1989.

with light in a new way. The collections of tableware, vases and lamps which Rigot designed in 1971 and 1972 in collaboration with Boris Tabacoff are a vivid reminder that crystal, like all glass, is in fact solidified liquid. The shapes of the pieces are fluid, watery, almost organic. While creating numerous other pieces for Baccarat, Rigot continued to develop the animal theme first embodied in his bronze sculptures, producing an owl in 1968, a penguin in 1971 and a hare in 1975. But he chose to work in abstract forms when creating sculptures for commemorative occasions. *De la Terre à la Lune* (From Earth to the Moon) pays homage to the Apollo programme for its exploration of the moon between 1968 and 1972. It was awarded the Gulbenkian Foundation's Grand Prix in Lisbon in 1972. *Terre et*

Cosmos (Earth and Cosmos), which incorporates the European flag taken to the moon by Apollo 16 in 1972, was presented by Baccarat to the Council of Europe in Strasbourg in 1974.

JEAN-FRANÇOIS ROBERT (born in Chantilly, 1778–1832). A decorative artist at the royal porcelain factory at Sèvres (1806–34 and 1836–43), Jean-François Robert also painted hunting scenes and landscapes for the Duc de Berry and the Grand Duchess of Tuscany and, above all, devoted his talents to the art of glassmaking, adapting the decorative processes he used on porcelain to glass and later to crystal. A contest was launched by the Société d'Encouragement in 1836 to promote France's glass industry, and in 1838 Robert won the prize for painted designs on glassware. To further his research, he worked closely with François-Eugène de Fontenay of the Plaine-de-Walsch glassworks in the Meurthe region, who shared his preoccupations. On 22 November 1837 Robert filed an application for a patent with the Ministry of Commerce and Public Works for the decoration of crystal using vitrifiable colours based on borosilicates, minium and metallic oxide colourings. Because crystal has a lower melting point than glass or porcelain, it cannot be annealed at the high temperatures needed to fix enamels. Robert's solution was to modify the composition of the polychrome enamels used to paint porcelain and colour glass for stained-glass windows, and adapt it to crystal by lowering the melting point of the enamels while maintaining their colouring capacity and their stability. The patent was granted in 1838 for ten years. In 1843 Robert, now working out of his own crystal-decorating workshop in Sèvres, entered into partnership with Jean-Baptiste Launay, manager of Launay, Hautin et Cie (which handled crystal sales after 1832 for the Baccarat, Saint-Louis, Choisy and Bercy crystalworks out of its Rue de Paradis headquarters in Paris). From 1843 to 1855 Robert decorated the opalines produced by Baccarat and Saint-Louis with magnificent floral motifs embellished with gold, silver and platinum, and was known to dilute his enamels with water, turpentine and, occasionally, even with essence of lavender.

ROBERTO SAMBONET (born in Vercelli, Italy, 1924). Roberto Sambonet studied architecture at the Politecnico in Milan and is a self-taught decorative artist and painter. His admiration for the Mediterranean, for its cultures, landscapes and people, has served as the inspiration for his watercolours and for the special sense of harmony that pervades Sambonet's work. A freelance designer since 1953, he has created jewelry for Tiffany's (United States) and porcelain for Bing & Grøndahl (Denmark) and

VÉSUVE (Vesuvius) caviar bowl, designed by Roberto Sambonet, 1972.

Richard Ginori (Italy), among others. He has also worked in book publishing as a graphic designer and art director. Since 1948 he has exhibited in Italy, Brazil and the United States. From 1971 to 1982 he collaborated with Baccarat as a designer and artistic consultant. Sambonet's work is characterized by a profound preoccupation with spatial relationships and the multiple ways in which the individual parts of a whole can interrelate. His *Angles* vases (1975) and *Tir* series for bars or table settings (1972) show how the mathematical interplay of objects can create new and startling juxtapositions which alter our regular perceptions of the world and arouse our imagination. Other pieces, like the caviar bowl *Vésuve* (Vesuvius; 1972), the *Préhistoire* (Prehistory) vases and *Vénus* (Venus) paperweights (1975), the *Aileron de Requin* (Shark's Fin) and *Queue de Thon* (Tuna Tail; 1982), serve to remind us of Sambonet's passion for Mediterranean forms and convey a natural sense of harmony.

BORIS TABACOFF (born in Dobrich, Bulgaria, 1927–85). Boris Tabacoff graduated from the Académie des Beaux-Arts in Paris. A freelance artist, he collaborated with Baccarat from 1970 to 1984, at first as a designer, then in connection with its arts department and auxiliary activities – designing window displays, setting up exhibition stands for the major international fairs (Bijorhca, Frankfurt), publishing catalogues and folding albums. Although he was not an avant-garde artist, the pieces he created in collaboration with Robert Rigot at the beginning of the 1970s were resolutely contemporary.

NICOLAS TRIBOULOT (born in Jeanmesnil, Vosges, 1963). Nicolas Triboulot, whose parents run a garden pottery business in the Vosges mountains, learned pottery techniques – shaping, firing and decorating – at the Lonchamp pottery workshop. He first came into contact with creative designs in ceramics at

VECTEUR (Vector) dish, designed by Nicolas
Triboulot, 1990.

the glazed earthenware factory at Rambervil-
liers in the Vosges, just fifteen kilometres (nine
miles) from Baccarat. Here he discovered old
plaster of Paris moulds which had been made
for artists from the Nancy school such as Louis
Majorelle (1859–1926) and Jacques Gruber
(1870–1936). In 1983 Baccarat hired the young
sculptor to work in its design department.
From the plaster of Paris sculptures he made
after models on paper, his experiments in
design, and his frequent visits to the workshops, Triboulot gradually learned all the
different techniques of crystal manufacturing.
In 1988 he asked permission to assist the
designer Thomas Bastide at Baccarat's head
office in Paris. After that things began to
happen very quickly. Triboulot's ideas had
been taking shape during the months of his
apprenticeship, and he now produced his
Vecteur (Vector) vase and bowl – models, he
says, that derive directly from his technical
knowledge, and whose production is the result
of a team effort.

CHARLES VITAL-CORNU (born in Paris, 1851–
1927). Charles Vital-Cornu worked with
plaster of Paris, marble and bronze, sculpting
in the round or creating decorative reliefs for
vases. He began exhibiting in 1874 and received
the Bronze Medal at the Exposition Universelle of 1889 for his decorative group *Belles
Vendanges* (Beautiful Harvests). Although his

style was classical, there is a liveliness to his
works which is conveyed by the titles, as in
Fierté Guerrière (Martial Pride; 1885), *Toréador*
(Toreador; 1888) and *Tendresse Humaine*
(Human Tenderness; 1905). The French
government presented *La Nature S'Eveille*
(Nature Awakes), a marble sculpture made in
1901, to the city of Aix-en-Provence. *Le Spleen*
(Spleen), another sculpture in marble dating
from 1897, is in the Musée de Peinture et de
Sculpture in Grenoble. Charles Vital-Cornu
was the ideal artist to design the nef in crystal
and bronze which symbolized the city of Paris
at the Exposition Universelle of 1900. The
work was produced by Baccarat and shown at
the exhibition by the Grand Dépôt department
store.

Other artists who have designed pieces pro-
duced by Baccarat in the twentieth century:
Lorentz Bäuner, Dominique Bonhomme,
César, Henri-Jean Closon, Douy-Pascault,
Aristide Colotte, Tauni de Lesseps, Katherine
de Sousa, Georges Dumaine, Olivier Gagnère,
Emile Gilioli, Gigi Guadagnucci, Claus A.
Harttung, Maréchal, Joindy and François Mor-
eau, Pascal Mourgue, Matei Negreanu, Joël
Rosenthal, Louis Süe, Van Day Truex, Marie-
Françoise Villepelet, Yan Zoritchak.

A HISTORY OF THE BACCARAT CRYSTALWORKS

1760 – The Rosières saltworks is shut down when saline levels fall due to the infiltration of lake water into the salt water. As a result, wood from the forests of the *châtellenie* of Baccarat, which belongs to the diocese of Metz, is no longer needed for fuel. His Grace Louis de Montmorency-Laval, Lord Bishop of Metz, expresses hopes of founding a 'furnace works' to replace the saltworks.

1764 – 16 October: Louis XV agrees to let the bishop found a glassworks in the *châtellenie* of Baccarat so as to provide work for local woodcutters and check the importation of glass from Bohemia into France.

1765 – The Bishop of Metz builds the glassworks near Baccarat, the largest market town in the *châtellenie*, on the banks of the River Meurthe, which serves to transport felled timber to the factory.
16 February: At his residence in Marly, Louis XV signs letters patent confirming his decision. The parliament of Metz registers the deed and limits the number of furnaces which can function simultaneously at the glassworks to three. The bishop appoints Antoine Renaut as director of the glassworks. Renaut's father was the director of the royal glassworks at Saint-Quirin, a temporal property of the prelate. The new glassworks is named 'Renaut et Compagnie'.

1766 – 11 June: The Bishop of Metz requests a major financial contribution from Léopold, Seigneur de Corny, and a three-member partnership is formed – between the bishop himself, Antoine Renaut and Léopold – which takes effect retroactively as of 1 January 1765, for a duration of twelve years. A fourth furnace is activated. The glassworks functions with two furnaces for the glassware, one for window glass, and one for 'table or Bohemian glass', which is, in fact, plate glass.

1768 – 30 July: The company's name is changed to 'Verreries de Baccarat' since Renaut is now only one of three partners.

1773 – 19 July: Following Léopold's death the partnership founded in 1766 is dissolved. Renaut purchases the remaining shares and becomes sole owner of the glassworks. He agrees to buy his wood from the Bishop of Metz, who accords him exclusive rights to his forests.

1775 – The company's name is changed to 'Verreries Sainte-Anne' (probably after the name of Renaut's mother).
A chapel, placed under the protection of Saint Anne, is built within the factory walls, and a priest is brought in to celebrate mass and reside on the premises.
Renaut succeeds in reducing by one third the amount of fuel needed for the furnaces. The result is a reduction in manufacturing costs and an increase in sales. The glassworks' products are sold throughout France, particularly in the ports exporting to Spain, Africa and America.

1789–1810 – Church possessions are declared State property. The glassworks no longer has exclusive rights to the forests owned by the diocese of Metz, and the price of fuel, sold by auction, rises drastically. Foreign markets shut down, including Spain, the French colonies and North America.

1790 – Sainte-Anne becomes a separate municipality from Baccarat, with its own mayor.

1802 – 17 December: Antoine Renaut, after thirty-seven years of responsibility at the glassworks, sells the factory to three of his eight children – Charles, Isidore and Pierre – while reserving the right to reside in the château adjoining the glassworks courtyard.

1806 – 12 December: Deeply in debt, Antoine Renaut's children declare bankruptcy and put the glassworks up for auction. It is purchased by Lippmann-Lippmann, a Verdun businessman. The town of Sainte-Anne is incorporated into the municipality of Baccarat.

1810–11 – The first hydraulically operated cutting machines are installed to replace the pedal-driven type previously used. Glass-cutting, however, only attains its full importance with the advent of crystal manufacturing.

1811 – Wood is so expensive and the demand for glass so small that one of the two functioning furnaces is extinguished.

1813 – Production is stopped. The factory is put up for sale.

1816 – 7 March: Louis XVIII signs an act granting the Vonêche glass- and crystalworks exemption from customs duties. Incorporated into Belgium under the treaty of 20 November 1815, the Vonêche factory, the property of

Aimé-Gabriel d'Artigues (1773–1848) since 1802, had lost its French clientele as a result. The king asks d'Artigues, a chemist and member of the Conseil Général des Manufactures de France, to found a crystalworks on French territory.

Of all the sites he visits, d'Artigues finds the 'Verreries Sainte-Anne' most to his liking because of its proximity to the Meurthe and because of the existence of the canal, built specially to bring the floating logs even closer to the factory.

15 May: The Lippmann-Lippmann glassworks is sold to Aimé-Gabriel d'Artigues.

15 November: Before even receiving the royal deed confirming the purchase, d'Artigues has the first crystal furnace lit and operating.

1817 – 9 April: A royal act gives d'Artigues the right to open his crystalworks in the 'Verreries Sainte-Anne'. The company's name becomes 'Verreries de Vonêche à Baccarat'. D'Artigues builds minium and sodium sulphate factories next to the crystalworks.

November: A second crystal furnace is activated.

1818 – March: A third crystal furnace is activated. D'Artigues stops crystal being exported from Vonêche to France.

1819 – Exposition Nationale des Produits de l'Industrie Française. Baccarat does not enter the competition because d'Artigues is a member of the jury. But Madame Désarnaud, director of the Escalier de Cristal department store in Paris, shows some Baccarat crystal created at the Palais-Royal workshops and receives a Gold Medal.

1822 – D'Artigues falls seriously ill. Because he still owes part of the purchase money to Lippmann-Lippmann, he decides to sell Baccarat to pay off his debt.

1823 – 7 January: Three partners – Pierre-Antoine Godard-Desmarest (a Parisian property owner), Lescuyer (a property owner from Mézières), and Lolot (a businessman from Charleville) – purchase d'Artigues's factory.

The workforce totals 327 workers, including 114 glass-blowers and 111 cutters.

Exposition Nationale des Produits de l'Industrie Française in Paris. Baccarat takes part for the first time, exhibiting clear and opal crystal, and wins a Gold Medal. (The award strictly belongs to d'Artigues.)

1824 – 14 February: The three partners decide to found a public company for a duration of twenty years, counting retroactively from January 1823. The company's name is changed to 'Compagnie des Verreries et Cristalleries de Vonêche-Baccarat'.

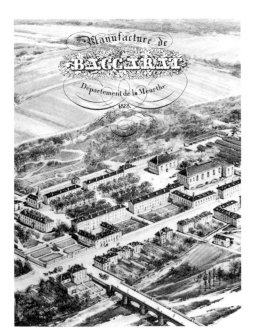

Bird's-eye view of the Baccarat glassworks in 1828, ink wash on heavy paper.

3 March: King Charles X gives his consent to the founding of a public company.

A new cutting workshop is built with a hundred machines run by hydraulic power. The Baccarat glass-blower Ismaïl Robinet invents a piston air pump to facilitate glass-blowing.

1825 – The technique of press-moulding is developed, producing moulded crystal imitations of blown crystal. Its rapid execution and low manufacturing cost promote sales among the middle classes, with the result that business begins to prosper.

1826 – 27 April: The company purchases the glass- and crystalworks in Trélon (Nord).

1827 – A school for workers' sons is opened at the crystalworks, with evening classes for adults.

Exposition Nationale des Produits de l'Industrie Française in Paris. Baccarat shows opaque crystal imitations of jasper and agate, created by Jean-Baptiste Toussaint, director of the factory, and receives a Gold Medal. But the current fashion is for light and transparent crystal, and the production of opaque crystal is soon abandoned for commercial reasons.

1828 – 26 February: An exclusive agreement is signed between Baccarat-Trélon and Fresne Barbier, a Parisian wholesaler specializing in products from a number of crystalworks including that of Saint-Louis in Moselle.

8 March: When Barbier fails to honour the exclusive agreement (continuing to sell Saint-Louis's products as well as those of Baccarat and Trélon), a second agreement is signed according to which products from Baccarat and Trélon are to make up three quarters of Barbier's stock.

12 September: King Charles X visits the Baccarat crystalworks.

1831 – 20 March: The revolution of 1830 causes severe financial difficulties. One of Baccarat's two furnaces is extinguished. At the Trélon factory, the only crystal furnace is extinguished and replaced by a simple glass-melting furnace.

7 October: A partnership is formed between Baccarat, Saint-Louis and a group of seven wholesale dealers in crystal with the purpose of founding the company of Barbier, Launay et Cie (Rue de Paradis-Poissonnière, Paris) for a duration of ten years as of 1 January 1832. Baccarat and Saint-Louis are to entrust all their crystal to the company, which pledges to sell it wholesale and exclusively. Baccarat welcomes the partnership as a means of creating a monopoly of the manufacturing and marketing of crystal in France. Baccarat holds the highest proportion of registered capital. The wholesalers Barbier and Launay handle the day-to-day management of the business.

14 Ocober: Georges Bontemps (1799–1884), director of the Choisy-le-Roi glass- and crystalworks, requests admission to the trust as of 1 January 1832. His request is accepted because of his remarkable abilities as a glass engineer, and an agreement is signed between Choisy-le-Roi and Barbier, Launay et Cie. Bontemps, a graduate of the Ecole Polytechnique, apparently worked for a brief period at Baccarat (probably in around 1820) before becoming director of Choisy-le-Roi.

November: Baccarat's second furnace is reactivated.

1832 – 9 July: The former crystalworks of Saint-Cloud, located in Montcenis near Le Creusot, finds itself in difficulties and is forced to cease manufacture between 1827 and October 1831. The firm's directors, the Chagot brothers, express their wish to enter the trust founded in 1831, but Baccarat refuses their request. Baccarat and Saint-Louis offer to buy the Montcenis crystalworks.

24 August: Following Barbier's death Barbier, Launay et Cie becomes Launay, Hautin et Cie.

1833 – 25 March: The small Bercy crystalworks joins the trust. Located on the outskirts of Paris, it can provide rapid manufacturing and delivery of urgent matching stock. A sales catalogue is published by Launay, Hautin et Cie showing products by Baccarat, Saint-Louis, Choisy-le-Roi and, later, Bercy.

1834 – Exposition Nationale des Produits de l'Industrie Française in Paris. Baccarat shows a variety of pieces in cut and moulded crystal, as well as individual parts for chandeliers, and wins a Gold Medal. The company has a workforce of seven hundred and is exporting to North and South America, Italy, Germany, Switzerland, Spain, etc.

1835 – Baccarat and Saint-Louis sell the Creusot crystalworks. A clause in the agreement prohibits the new owner from manufacturing crystal for fifty years. Baccarat activates a third furnace and takes on a number of glassmakers from the Creusot factory.

To compete with ordinary glassworks like Plaine-de-Walsch, which produces a very white, press-moulded glass imitating crystal but less expensive, Baccarat launches new moulded designs in the neo-Gothic style.

An insurance scheme is started for glass-cutters, providing sickness benefits for those on sick leave. The scheme is only available to those glass-cutters not provided with free housing in the factory grounds.

1836 – 7 May: A second furnace is activated at Trélon, for the manufacture of moulded glass. A new glass-cutting workshop is built at Deneuvre, near Baccarat.

1837 – September: Following Saint-Louis's example, and on the recommendation of Jean-Baptiste Launay, Baccarat begins producing amber-coloured glass. Other types of coloured glass and, later, coloured crystal follow.

1838 – Exposition des Produits de l'Industrie Française in Nancy. Baccarat shows cut and moulded pieces in clear crystal, opal crystal and coloured glass (turquoise, black and amber-tinted).

July–August: Emile Godard-Desmarest (son of Pierre-Antoine) and Jean-Baptiste Toussaint travel to Germany and Bohemia to visit a number of glassworks that manufacture coloured and decorated glass. An engraver and a glass-cutter are hired to work at Baccarat.

1839 – The engraver and glass-cutter arrive from Bohemia.

Baccarat now employs a total of 1,000 workers, of whom 402 are glass-cutters, 208 glass-blowers, and 3 engravers, with an increase in the number of glass-cutters compared to that of glass-blowers.

Exposition Nationale des Produits de l'Industrie Française in Paris. Baccarat exhibits its new neo-Gothic moulded pieces and articles decorated with Chinese and Japanese motifs, in coloured crystal (light green, amethyst, pink, purple and orange-tinted) and engraved in Bohemian style. It wins a Gold Medal.

1840 – 15 February: The repercussions of the financial crisis in the United States cause a drop in production. The third furnace is extinguished.
One, then two water turbines are linked up to the glass-cutting workshop.
The Trélon factory is leased to its director, Hyppolithe Godard-Desmarest, for an annual rental fee, and on the condition that the factory never manufactures crystal or even imitation-crystal moulded glass, but only ordinary glass.

1841 – January: François-Eugène de Fontenay arrives at Baccarat to give support to Jean-Baptiste Toussaint. The duration of the melting and refining processes is regulated using procedures perfected by Fontenay at the Plaine-de-Walsch and Wallérysthal glassworks. Glassworkers are henceforth able to work to regular timetables.

1842 – 12 April: King Louis-Philippe agrees to extend the life of the public company for forty years as of 1 January 1843. New capital is issued and the company's name becomes 'Compagnie des Verreries et Cristalleries de Baccarat'.

1844 – Exposition Nationale des Produits de l'Industrie Française. Baccarat shows crystal of a regular 'whiteness' (limpidity and transparency) thanks to François-Eugène de Fontenay's improvements. Also shown are the first pieces in white imitation-porcelain opal crystal, in dichroic yellow crystal obtained with uranium oxide and in variously coloured agate glass. Baccarat receives a Gold Medal.

1845 – 15 May–15 July: Exhibition of Austrian Industrial Products in Vienna. Jean-Baptiste Toussaint, accompanied by Antoine Seiler, director of the Saint-Louis crystalworks, and Eugène Péligot, professor at the Conservatoire National des Arts et Métiers, attends the exhibition and brings the idea of millefiori paperweights back to France.

1846 – Baccarat begins making paperweights.

1847 – The Choisy-le-Roi glass- and crystalworks shuts down due to financial difficulties. Georges Bontemps leaves for England and takes over the direction of a glassworks in Birmingham. In 1867 he publishes an important *Guide du verrier* (Glassworker's Guide), and in 1876 he translates the manuscript written by the monk Theophilus (eleventh–twelfth centuries) on the art of making glass.

1848 – The revolution and the ensuing financial crisis force the Bercy crystalworks to shut down. The factory continues to produce ordinary glass. Baccarat and Saint-Louis are now the only members of the trust.
20 March: Only one furnace remains in activity at Baccarat. Working hours are reduced and the workers receive unemployment compensation until normal activity resumes.

1849 – A railway link is built between Strasbourg and Paris. Delivery of crystal from Baccarat to Paris now takes only three days instead of the ten required for transportation by road. However, this also increases competition with other French crystalworks.
Exposition Nationale des Produits de l'Industrie Française in Paris. Baccarat shows vases with handles and moulded medallions, paperweights and pieces decorated with filigreework, and wins a Gold Medal.

1851 – 15 September: A pension scheme is started for glass-cutters, engravers and gilders.

1852 – The economy picks up, coinciding with the establishment of the Second Empire. Three furnaces are working at Baccarat. A total of seven furnaces will be in operation before the recession of the 1880s forces further cutbacks.

1853 – A chemist's position is created at the crystalworks. The chemist, whose job is to experiment with colours and make sure that the raw materials used are of the highest quality, reports to the factory director.

1853–54 – Baccarat experiments with the English method of steam coal heating, but it proves more expensive than using wood.

1855 – Second Exposition Universelle in Paris. Baccarat exhibits two candelabra (height: 5.25 m/17 ft) of 90 candlesticks each, a large chandelier (height: 4.85 m/16 ft) and collections of agate glass, clear, opal and coloured crystal, with painted motifs, gilding, filigree-work and occasionally bronze. It wins a Gold Medal.

Oil and vinegar bottles and salt-cellar in blue-cased cut crystal with silver-plated bronze stand.

The chemist L. Kessler succeeds in manufacturing hydrofluoric acid in sufficient quantities for use on an industrial scale.
Due to conflicts with the personnel, Jean-Baptiste Launay leaves the trust.

1857 – 24 June: The partnership linking Baccarat and Saint-Louis is finally dissolved after interminable discussions over production and market shares.
The real estate of Launay, Hautin et Cie is divided up between Baccarat and Saint-Louis. Baccarat opens its own warehouse in Paris.

1858 – Jean-Baptiste Toussaint dies.

1859 – The pension scheme is extended to include all categories of workers at Baccarat. The total Baccarat workforce stands at 1,480 employees.

1860 – A series of free-trade treaties forces Baccarat to face international competition now that foreign-made products can be imported freely into France.

1864 – Baccarat acquires the procedure of etching called 'Venetian engraving', which uses acid to obtain a hollow, frosted impression. Thanks to the procedures discovered by Kessler in 1854 and 1855, the crystalworks now has all the necessary techniques at its disposal for developing etching on crystal.

1867 – Exposition Universelle in Paris. Baccarat shows a fountain (height: 7.3 m/24 ft), engraved vases and bowls by Jean-Baptiste Simon, pieces in etched and painted crystal and cased crystal, and an assortment of other pieces inspired by Etruscan, Greek, Egyptian, Venetian, Renaissance and eighteenth-century art.

1868 – A school is opened at the crystalworks for the daughters of workers.

1874 – 2 November: The Trélon glassworks is sold to Charles Cuvillier, director of the factory since July 1873.

1876 – A railway link is opened between Lunéville and Saint-Dié, facilitating the transportation of wood throughout the region but increasing the number of buyers. Baccarat experiments with steam coal heating again.

1878 – Exposition Universelle in Paris. Baccarat exhibits a temple (height: 5 m/16 ft) housing a reproduction of Giambologna's *Flying Mercury* (Florence, sixteenth century). It also shows a collection of engraved pieces that replicate works in rock crystal held in the Louvre. Despite winning a Gold Medal, Baccarat is attacked by the critics for its lack of strong artistic direction.

1882 – The last wood furnace is extinguished at Baccarat. All the furnaces are now coal-fired.

Baccarat's bronze workshop on Rue de Paradis.

1885 – The workforce at Baccarat totals 2,340 employees.

1886 – A warehouse is opened in Bombay. Closed in 1888, it is reopened in 1892. Other warehouses are opened in South America.

Bird's-eye view of the Baccarat works in 1907.

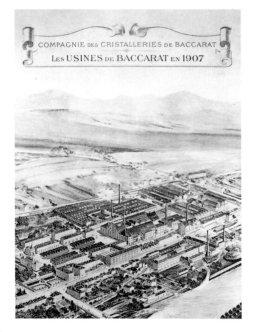

COMPAGNIE DES CRISTALLERIES DE BACCARAT
LES USINES DE BACCARAT EN 1907

1887 – Baccarat takes part *hors concours* in an exhibition in Hanoi.
The workforce is reduced to 2,073 employees as a result of the particularly severe financial crisis of 1885–87.

1889 – Exposition Universelle in Paris. Instead of exhibiting its crystalwork, Baccarat gives a presentation of its social policies on behalf of the workers.

Baccarat-Christofle pavilion at the Exposition Internationale des Arts Décoratifs in 1925. Architect: Georges Chevalier.

1890 – To protect the workers from the vagaries of the economy, Comte Aldebert de Chambrun, the company's main shareholder, advocates unemployment benefits consisting of payments made solely by the establishment.

1892 – An import agency for Baccarat crystal is opened in New York.

1896 – A gilding workshop is set up at the warehouse in Rue de Paradis. The bronze workshop on Boulevard Beaumarchais is transferred to Rue de Paradis.

1898 – An additional cutting workshop is opened in Bertrichamps, near Baccarat, to create chandeliers and perfume bottles.
A telephone line is opened between Lunéville and Baccarat, allowing direct contact with the Paris warehouse.

Baccarat's retail shop in New York, c. 1960.

1899 – In his will Aldebert de Chambrun bequeaths a number of his shares, including interest and dividends, to the workers as a profit-sharing scheme.

1900 – Exposition Universelle in Paris. As in 1889, Baccarat presents its social policies rather than exhibiting its crystal. But the Grand Dépôt department store shows some Baccarat creations, notably the large crystal and bronze nef.
Sales of Baccarat crystal increase on the export market in the United States, the East and Russia. Four furnaces are now functioning.

Interior of the Baccarat-Christofle pavilion, 1925.

1984 – The Baccarat Pacific affiliate is set up in Tokyo.

1986 – The third tank furnace is installed at Baccarat.
Baccarat and Henri Addor & Associés publish *Baccarat, les flacons à parfum, répertoire du collectionneur* (Baccarat's Perfume Bottles: A Collector's Catalogue).

1989 – Baccarat celebrates its 225th anniversary. The workforce totals 1,060 employees.
18 January: René de Chambrun presents President Ronald Reagan with a paperweight containing a sulphide of George Washington and the Marquis de La Fayette based on a medallion issued by the National Mint in Paris in 1931 to celebrate the 150th anniversary of the victory of Yorktown. A second copy of the paperweight is given to Vice-President George Bush.
15 June: On the occasion of his admission to the Académie Française, Commander Jacques-Yves Cousteau is given the traditional academician's sword with pommel and tang by Baccarat.
12 August: The Kanemori Museum opens in the historic port of Hakodate in Japan. Its collections are composed exclusively of Baccarat pieces, including a twenty-three-piece service reissued in 1986.
6 October: Baccarat opens its second Paris boutique, Baccarat-Madeleine, in the building of the former Vase Etrusque, a shop located on Boulevard Malesherbes and then, from 1861, on Place de la Madeleine.

1990 – 9 January: There is a press launch for Baccarat's new collection at the Musée de la Marine, Place du Trocadéro, Paris, to celebrate its 'blue period' and the revival of coloured crystal with works in cobalt-blue crystal.
12 October: The exhibition 'Baccarat, Tradition et Création' (Baccarat, Tradition and Creation) opens at the Salon des Antiquaires de Marseille. The exhibition includes pieces from the Musée Baccarat (located on Rue de Paradis in Paris), a homage to Georges Chevalier and work designed by contemporary artists for Baccarat.
Christmas: A giant-sized Christmas tree, designed by the Danish architect Claus A. Harttung and produced by Baccarat, is erected on the square in front of the Madeleine church for the Christmas period. The metal framework is decorated with 2,500 crystal pieces forming sixteen giant snowflakes.

ACKNOWLEDGMENTS

·:·

The publishers would like to thank Jean-Louis Curtis, Véronique Nansenet and Jacques Boulay, the authors and photographers of the present volume.
They are also deeply grateful to M. René de Chambrun, Chairman of Baccarat, for the confidence he has placed in them by encouraging the publication of this book.

Heartfelt thanks are also owing to the following: Pierre Ayral, Patrick Baboin, Michel Bacus, Christian Balma, Françoise Birck, Léon Boutteville, Chantal Burns, Roland Chevalier, Gérard Cornier, Paul-André Coulbois, Isabelle d'Hauteville, Henri Jeanjean, Michel Joannes, Dominique Lécuyer, Ginette Leroux, Denis Mangin, Yves du Petit Thouars, Marie-Madeleine Perreaut, André Pichard, François Renaud, François Satger, Louis Satler, Lydie Sébire, the Galerie Suger, Michel Treger.

Particular thanks go to the following museums for their help: Chrysler Museum, Norfolk, Virginia; Corning Museum of Glass, Corning, New York; Los Angeles Museum of Art, Los Angeles, California; Musée des Arts Décoratifs, Paris; Musée Baccarat, Paris; Musée Baccarat, Baccarat; Musée du Conseil de l'Europe, Strasbourg; Musée International de la Parfumerie, Grasse; Musée Louis-Philippe, Eu; Musée National des Arts et Techniques, Paris; Musée Océanographique de Monaco, Monte Carlo.

PHOTO CREDITS

·:·

JACQUES BOULAY. Pages: 2, 6, 8, 9, 10, 11, 12, 13, 14, 15, 16, 17, 18, 19, 20, 21, 22, 23, 24, 26, 27, 28, 29, 30, 31, 32, 33, 34, 35, 36, 37, 38, 39, 84, 85, 100, 101, 102, 103, 106, 107, 108, 109, 110, 111, 112, 114, 115, 116, 117, 118, 119, 120, 121, 122, 123, 124, 125, 126, 127, 128, 129, 131, 132, 133, 134, 135, 136, 137, 138, 141, 142, 143, 144, 145, 147, 148, 149, 150, 151, 153, 154, 155, 156, 157, 158, 161, 162, 163, 166, 167, 168, 169, 170, 171, 172, 173, 174, 175, 178, 180, 182, 185, 189, 191, 193, 195, 196, 198, 199, 200, 201, 202, 205, 206, 207, 210, 211, 212, 213, 214, 215, 216, 217, 218, 219, 220, 221, 223, 227, 230, 231, 232, 233, 234, 235, 236, 237, 238, 239, 240, 241, 246, 247, 250, 251, 253, 254, 255, 256, 257, 258, 259, 260, 261, 262, 263, 264, 266, 267, 268, 269, 270, 271, 272, 273, 275, 276, 277, 287.

CORNING MUSEUM OF GLASS. Page: 183.

CLAUDE FRAYARD. Pages: 24, 87, 91, 92, 93, 181, 184, 244, 274, 287, 299.

FRANÇOISE RESIN. Pages: 82, 88, 89, 105, 160, 177, 186, 187, 188, 190, 194, 197, 203, 204, 222, 224, 226, 248, 249, 252, 260, 265.

STUDIO 122. Pages: 165, 225.

STUDIO KOLLAR. Page: 298.

JEAN-MICHEL TARDY. Pages: 98, 99, 100, 101, 130, 134, 135, 137, 138, 139, 152, 159, 161, 166, 167, 174, 175, 178, 195, 198, 199, 202, 205, 216, 217, 250, 251, 256, 257, 266, 267, 268, 269.